Italic —— What gives *Typography* its emphasis

Hendrik Weber

niggli

Imprint

The Deutsche Nationalbibliothek lists this publication in the
Deutsche Nationalbibliografie; detailed bibliographic data are available
on the Internet at http://dnb.dnb.de

Translation: Dan Reynolds
Editing /Proofreading: Sandra Ellegiers
Graphic design: Hendrik Weber, Paulina Pysz
Typeface: Typeby Lirico (designed by Hendrik Weber)

ISBN 978-3-7212-1009-5

© 2021 Niggli, imprint of Braun Publishing AG, Salenstein

www.niggli.ch

1st English edition 2021

...entes de

Revues

RFA USA Projections

et Ventes

Guides annonces

DVD

Revues contacts K7

Lingerie Cuir TOUS

Latex Gadgets SYSTEMES

PAL

Aphrodisiaques

SECAM

Elle Bai NTSC

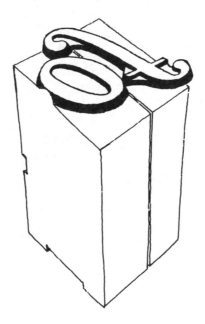

01 {p.3} Neon lettering in Paris   02 {↑} Two italic printing sorts with one kern

Table of contents

mh **italic**

03 unconnected,
   left-leaning

mh *italic*

04 connected,
   upright

mh *italic*

05 unconnected,
   right-leaning

....

Introduction

Although typography essentially consists of a rhythmic sequence of black and white surfaces, it was the 'grey areas' that aroused my interest in this exciting subject. Italic typefaces are one of those grey areas. Taking a closer look at them, vyou quickly notice that there is a general lack of clarity about their appearance. In typography, the interrelationships of forms are normally determined by how the letters look. At the same time, other aspects are relevant, which is why definitions can vary. On the one hand, typography has established rules for italics, according to which 'italic' faces have designs that result from cursive writing. On the other hand, this concept of a typographically 'true' italic loses its relevance outside discipline-specific contexts. Public discourse ignores the above-mentioned facts, preferring simplified ideas about what an italic is or is not. After all, a text's content should be in the foreground, not the presentation of a specific typeface. This makes it not surprising that – from the reader's point of view – an italic's slope is what catches the eye. Which of these two positions is correct and which is false? What is genuine and what is (un)authentic?

Those differences are based, among other things, on the various standards set within typography. Traditional typefaces like *Times* are standard fonts today; that also applies to the associated *Times Italic,* whose character is independent. A second category consists of typefaces like *Univers* or *Arial,* whose italics look like oblique versions of their upright styles. Both methods represent fundamentally different ideas of how italic letterforms should be constructed.

How should type designers respond to this? Is the decisive characteristic of an italic the degree of slant its letterforms have, or is it the construction of the letterforms? Does one characteristic prevent the other?

To offer some insight into this problem, I would like to make a comparison using the examples to the left. The three word-images illustrate how much of their 'italic' definitions remain when the features enumerated above are applied in isolation.

As I see it, none of the word-images has the desired character of a *true italic* – neither the two outer ones nor the example in the middle. Why not? This can be explained in detail as follows: first, we see two different types of letter-form construction. Both outer-most words are defined as 'italics' because of their interrupted construction. The word in the middle, however, has an *uninterrupted* construction. On the other hand, the word in the middle lacks direction, while the neighbouring words slope to the left and right.

The first word (left-leaning) appears to be readable, but in my eyes is still not very legible. Due to its rarity, this atypical slope does not correspond to typographic conventions, limiting the reading comfort it offers. Its counterpart at the bottom seems more familiar because of the inclination to the right. Yet according to typographical rules, this example would have to be described as a 'fake italic', just like the upper-most word.

That leaves us with the word in the middle, whose connected writing style reveals its true construction. But many would consider its lack of a slope a shortcoming.

A single feature in-and-of-itself only has half the potential needed to fully realise the italic form. Consequently, a 'true' italic can only be the result of several factors. It is neither 'just connected' nor exclusively 'just inclined'. Instead it could be both sloped and connected at the same time, and various other formal characteristics could play a role, too.

The purpose of this demonstration is to illustrate the limits of the formal italic structure. One of the main tasks of this book is to illustrate these descriptions, visualise them, and later incorporate them into a general definition.

To be able to answer the questions raised above, it is important to thoroughly look at the history of writing, because every written and printed text is the result of a complex process of developments in writing itself. For example, in the early phase of italics' creation, around 1500, some typefaces inclined slightly and had a cursive character.[1] Today, however, almost no sans serif typefaces use that structure; they are purely static and slanted. But there are also more traditional ideas – so-called 'standards' of typography – that consider oblique letterforms deficient. What consequences does this cause when considering the future variants that italic typefaces could take?

Is it possible to draw lessons from history for designing italics? Or should we ignore tradition and just look forward? How much flexibility should a definition include? This book attempts to systematically explore these interelated issues. It was precisely in this spirit that the book's sequence of contents came about: the first part studies fundamental questions about italic typefaces themselves. The second part traces the historical development of the 'italic' style to find out the basis of italic typefaces' designs and to investigate which features ultimately make up the italic character.

....

Cursive's role in typography

An italic typeface's quality results from the interplay of technical-functional aspects with purely aesthetic ones, which can vary a great deal based on the area of intended use and the requirements on the typeface.

Design professionals rely on italics' distinctiveness to effectively empha-sise particular text passages. In doing so, they make specific demands on italics' forms, for which they draw on their historical development.

This perception – viewed as *traditional* – is not particularly noticed. Instead, an impression revealing a completely different, more technical perspective has taken root, which deviates from the historically conditioned italics. Both points of view are typographically justified and must be paid attention to when formulating this subject.

Furthermore, a great deal of written and printed artefacts have come down to us from the history of letters. We can now consider a high proportion of them to have used cursive forms. To keep track of these, typographers have found that *classifying* them by name is unavoidable. Since there often seem to be multiple terms available that describe the same thing, a closer investiga-tion is necessary.

General development

Each letter of any typeface meant to be taken seriously is related to handwriting, to some degree. By this, I refer to forms written with a pen or other similar tool. In most italic fonts, these handwritten roots are more pronounced than in other typefaces. The development of writing is of particular importance here.

Over the last several centuries, writing became an omnipresent part of our civilization*. It served to record knowledge and educational content in the sciences, culture and religion. Because of this important function, certain expec-tations for written forms have been maintained. These provided the basis for model cursive styles to develop. With the increasing influence of technology in everyday life, the aesthetic demands placed on writing began to fall. Although that decline has not been continuous, it is nevertheless a process that is happening step by step. Today, there is even the danger that the making of

....
{←} Until the 1970s, slate boards and chalk were still used for schools' writing and arithmetic lessons.

*According to Noordzij, stern civilization is 'the ltural community that avails itself of western writing.'**2**

handwritten documents will disappear completely, and the original reference
point for italic typefaces will thus be lost.

This trend is already noticeable in schools. Penmanship is only taught until
children can write on their own. When I was growing up in Germany, we practised a fixed model of cursive handwriting called the *Schulausgangsschrift*, while
children in some neighbouring states learnt a similar 'simplified connected
script' called the *Vereinfachte Ausgangsschrift*. The details of the forms used in
handwriting styles in my country derive from these models. In the meantime,
ballpoint pens have replaced metal nibs; keyboards brought added comfort.
The latter has another (apparent) advantage: absolute control over an easily
readable text.

We live in a time when it is faster to type a word than to write it by hand.
Using prefabricated letters, this can be done more comfortably, beautifully and
wonderfully on the monitor. On top of that, we can even do it in colour. When
filling out a form, or when writing a note or a shopping list, the aesthetic aspect
of handwriting is becoming ever more seldom. One of the its remaining uses
is perhaps for signing documents.

As history teaches us, 'serious' letters will stick around in the media world;
by that, I mean on computers and in magazines, books, signs advertising things,
logos, etc. It is interesting to note that the traditional forms used by early
printers from the *incunabula** period have survived almost unchanged to the
present day. They even represent a certain kind of 'standard' for book typefaces,
even though we do not have a historical connection to them.

* *Incunabula* is the term
used to describe the
first 50 years of
printing with move-
able metal type.

Almost no differences are visible between historical typefaces and those used today, although four hundred years lie between them.

....

7 A humanist cursive written by Arrighi, 1523

8 The *Monotype Blado* typeface from 1926 is almost identical to the original model

baegn

09 A postcard written by someone who was clearly ambitious, 1897

Espresso

10   The well-known italic button used for emphasising content within a text may be found on the menu bar in MS-Word. If the program does not find a suitable italic font, the selected text will automatically be slanted by 12 degrees, even if the typeface used is already cursive in style.

We type texts into our laptops and use fonts whose roots go back about five hundred years.

Their designs come from a time when electricity did not yet exist. Nevertheless, the application of these typefaces is part of everyday life – no matter what or how much we might know about them. Unlike professionals, the general public only has a very basic understanding of typography. If I carried out a general survey on the characteristics of italics, the answers would probably be rather simple:

word → *slant* → *italic.*

11   {→} Window lettering on a bistro in Brussels featuring both upright and slanted cursive letters, 2004

Champig

Carott

Saumon - Broc

Champignons sa

Carottes au

Mille feuilles

Assiettes

Nos plats sont a

RESTAURANT

Bulletin

BCC

VISA

mignons

ottes

ocolis - Poireaux

sauvages & lardons

u cumin

es d'aubergines

es froides

aussi à emporter

....

Typographic significance

We owe the preservation and transmission of letterform-related traditions
to professional printers, lithographers, engravers, typesetters and typographers.
They gave italics a special status. The discourse here is about the typographical
link to the Roman alphabet. This relationship between *roman* and *italic*
is historically conditioned since both styles have common roots, particularly
in the variations on the *Carolingian minuscule* practised in the 9th century.

In the 15th century, Italian humanists revived these and merged them with
the capitals *(Capitalis Monumentalis)* that the Romans used for monumental
inscriptions in stone. In this way, the so-called humanist writing style came
into being. Shortly after its introduction around 1400, however, its implemention
split in two different directions: *connected* and *unconnected*.

In the beginning, the difference between the *humanist minuscule* (interrupted) and the cursive lowercase (uninterrupted) was still minimal, since they
shared a common calligraphic origin. This changed shortly after both styles
were adopted into typography.

While printers like Nicolas Jenson (1420 – 1480) drew the *humanist minuscule* nearer to the Roman *Capitalis*, cursive letters in metal type continued
to develop with a handwritten character. In this way, remarkable differences
developed between the forms present in each style, which typography still takes
advantage of today. When reading Renaissance texts, we receive two different
impressions: on the one hand, there is the upright roman, which looks printed
simply because of its rigidity. On the other hand, the italic suggests a written
image, because of its free form.[3]

The slightly narrower proportions of italic lower-case letters led (through
the work of Aldus Manutius) to its temporary status as a text typeface with
which even whole books could be printed. Although this practice lasted for some
time, it did not hold out permanently.

At the same time, the use of roman type also spread, whose static proportions dominate *(primary)* texts today, while the dynamic italics are used when
(secondary) emphasis is needed. Such a distribution of roles is undisputed
today and type users accept it as a given.

Whether a text typeface is italic or upright – as a type designer I see both
as having equal value. However, the freedom of every typeface is limited by
conventions.[4] There are no upright typefaces based on italics. Even type designers
must submit to this convention and use an upright style as the essential point of
reference for a new italic design. It is also important to remember that the
typographic tradition of the last two hundred years cannot be supplanted,
and in this time italic emphasis proved to be an irreplaceable typographic tool.
From the reader's point of view, a role reversal between italic and upright

typefaces would have profound consequences. The informational hierarchy that they are accustomed to when reading would be in complete disorder. The italic's autonomy also manifests itself through its function. This means that the present ranking (romans first, italics second) is binding.

According to typographical rules, italics are used in printed books – as well as on text pages – for the following elements:

- prefaces
- the emphasis of single words
- the distinguishing of quotations
- comments
- introductions
- indexes

To emphasise a text typographically means that specific parts and sections are set off from the rest. This provides more structure and encourages non-linear reading. The text will thus be easier for the reader to grasp.

Since comparable alternatives did not prevail, *italicisation* became the most popular method for creating emphasis. Until the 1980s, for instance, it was still common practice in Germany to simply accentuate texts by applying tracking*. This method was a relic from earlier times when most German texts were still composed with blackletter typefaces.[5]

According to points of view like having familiar-looking text settings, this method – and ones similar to it – can foretell the desired result. There is still a significant difference between separating a quotation from the main text by a change in typeface or through underlining, for instance. A typeface change in a text has a pleasant side-effect: it attracts attention and gives the reader a different perspective. For example, passages can maybe be given a specific voice or even their own look. This makes reading more attractive. Graphic designers and typographers know about these advantages, and others that are similar; they use these idiosyncrasies daily when dealing with texts. They choose the typeface and can to tell the difference between 'true' italics and 'fake' *(oblique)* ones.

*Tracking is the widening of the amount of space between all the characters in a word.

Some even feel committed to traditional values. But this was not always so. I would like to remind you of the Bauhaus era when every tradition was thrown overboard in favour of modernity. Italics were also adapted to these kinds of trends. In the end, only slanted versions of typefaces that had originated as upright designs existed. Additionally, the parallel development of some sans serif typefaces further reinforced the oblique formal characteristics of italics. Even today, the italics of many sans serif typefaces are 'only' obliqued. After a while, the trend of slanting typefaces began to fade and traditional italics found their way back onto paper; however, many oblique variants still remained.

In the meantime, typography has performed a balancing act by combining modern and traditional forms. Italics fulfil a typographic mission. They have to stand out clearly from the typeface used for the main text, without invalidaing it. For this reason, italic forms today are not only dependent on the zeitgeist but in particular on their upright counterpart's design.

The slant to the right is perhaps not a qualitative characteristic, except that it guarantees the function of emphasising. In turn, shape-related changes to the appearance of the text also provide the reader with added semantic value, which sometimes leads to more visually satisfying results. Taking typographical norms into account, a possible formula could be:

$$word \rightarrow slant \rightarrow (connected) \rightarrow italic$$

Diversity in palaeography

Cursive letters have various descriptions. For example, in palaeography – the science studying the styles and methods of writing from antiquity and modernity – they are grouped within practices of 'connected writing'.[6] The rather general, five-volume edition of the current (German) *Brockhaus* encyclopedia describes 'italics' as follows: '[lat.] (cursive) letters that slant to the right'.[7] However, 'italic' typefaces are not limited to one way of writing or being slanted. A specific relationship to an upright typeface should also be taken into account.

Upright and italic typefaces mutually depend on each other. Without upright typefaces, there would be no italics – and without italics, the options a designer would have when laying out a text would be rather limited. A modern typeface should have at least one italic, as a minimum. The number of italics was also connected with the increasing formal variety of upright text typefaces. This adaptive behaviour to any typeface construction testifies to italics' quality. At the same time, it is also the reason italics are difficult to classify into a particular category or group.

....

The roots of the word 'cursive' date back to antiquity. The Italian word *corsiva* was based on the Classical Latin *cursum,* which led to the Latin expression *currere*. In the literal sense, this can be translated as *running* or *hastening*. In contrast to the *Capitalis,* or the style of lettering used in Roman monumental inscriptions, most slanted cursives were intended for short-term use. These *vernacular styles* allowed for quick and uncomplicated writing. The required tools for the *Capitalis* were stone and a chisel, while cursive writing only needed papyrus and a reed pen, or a stylus and wax tablet.[8] Already in Cicero's day, an ancient form of shorthand was developed to record speeches in real-time, which is known as *Tironian notes*.

By the way, the word 'cursive' does not refer to either or writing or printing entirely. Since their adoption into typography in the early 16th century, informal styles of writing have been reproducible in letterpress printing without their construction having to be changed; even in printed form, the shapes of letters – although rigid and immovable – appear to be determined by the writing tool.[9]

In his standard text *The stroke. Theory of writing,* Gerrit Noordzij describes typography as 'writing with prefabricated letters'. Accordingly, italics can be considered both as *handwritten* as well as *printed*.[10] In this sense, the term 'cursive' designates the external result of a formal principle and is independent of the hand-making process.

There are cursive offshoots that have been developed because of historical correlations. Terms like *Italics, Oblique* and *Slanted* are included here, as well as *Scripts* and other connected cursive styles like the old German *Kurrent*. Regional and linguistic differences in terminology lead to additional confusion. The following list should help us to roughly classify this terminological grab bag. Afterwards, I provide a suggestion for the use of these different terms.

1.   As a technical term, *Italics* may be translated as *Italiken* (German) or *Italique* (French). Even though italics and cursives are related and the styles each originated within the same approximate geographical area of Italy, the terms came about at different times. *Italic* as a term was first used in 15th century England, instead of in Italy itself. The new handwriting style had spread from the southern side the Alps over Western Europe and across the English Channel. When the English came into contact with it, they named it after the country where the style had originated.[11] Its technical name was *Chancery,* referring to its use in Italy for documents produced inside various chanceries. Another writing style technically known as *Cancellaresca* was developed by court calligraphers who were so-called 'writing masters'. One of the most influential writing masters was Ludovico degli Arrighi, who also went by the

12   Italic

13   Cursive

name Ludovico Vincentino. It is assumed that the first handwriting described
as being *Italic* to arrive in Britain was his. At the beginning of the 16th century,
the *Cancellaresca* served as the house calligraphic style inside the papal chancery. Nevertheless, its narrow-looking design – written with the broad nib – was
already being adopted into typefaces for use in letterpress printing as early as
the 15th century. The style has served as the starting point for various impotant
 typefaces ever since.

2.   *Cursive* (lat. *currere* = to run) has been used as a term since the beginning
of the 17th century. It was used less often to describe sophisticated styles used
in book-making and more often to describe writing styles found in day-to-day
communication, as well as in *vernacular* and *official* texts. It derived from the
Italic, out of which many styles were developed.

In Germany, *Kurrent* cursive handwriting was in use until the middle of
the 20th century. Its appearances was very much influenced by the individ-
uality of person writing it, and therefore *Kurrent* really refers to a whole range
of styles. An overarching characteristic is that these styles were written with
pens that had pointed nibs, which is why they were also often called pointed
writing. Methods of writing *Kurrent* were taught in German primary schools
for more than a century, until they were replaced by more recent styles of
connecting scripts – i.e., the *Schulausgangsschrift* and the *Vereinfachte Ausgangsschrift*, etc., depending on the state. With the abandonment of the *vernacular*
handwriting styles previously used in business, as well as the *official* styles used
for bureaucratic paperwork, the term *Kurrent* disappeared completely.

It was already common practice in the 18th century to precisely mimic handwriting with printed typefaces. These imitations of handwriting styles are
called *scripts* (lat. writing). In his book on typeface classification, *Einteilung
der Druckschriften,* Georg Kurt Schauer wrote that – in contrast to italics – *scripts*
preserve individual characteristics more easily. [12] However, the differences
between *scripts* and italics are still difficult to define.

hh hh

Rafrivole
Rafrivole

....

14   Left-leaning italics   15   Italics with alternate letterforms,
                                                  or so-called 'traditional elements'

In most cases, these characteristics are limited to details like loops, knots or
connected letters. For as many kinds of handwriting as have existed and
are still practised, *script* typefaces in multiple variations may be found today.[13]
They are often used on greeting cards, certificates or advertisements.

3.   *Left-leaning italics* are only of marginal importance. Their origins point to
different areas of use, such as when more than one level of emphasis was needed. The most important area of application is in cartography. It is well-known
that *left-leaning italics* were used to indicate the names of rivers, for instance.
The advertising industry also made use of this style to achieve particularly power-
ful effects. Sometimes, it can be still be found on posters and in other advertising
materials.
        When it comes to handwriting, left-leaning styles are much more common.
However, this is not so much the product of a specific model being followed as
it is the result of individual writing practices.

4.   *Oblique* or *Slanted* is a group of styles that originated in the 19th century
under the influence of drawn lithographic 'fake' cursives. While 'true' italics
contain the basic characteristics of the style in terms of structure and form,
'fake' ones are reduced to only having the key feature of being slanted.[14]
        In this context, the term *sloped roman* must be mentioned. It refers to
upright typeface designs that have been slanted. In the middle of the 1930s,
traditional italics temporarily fell out of fashion. The angle was seen as the

h*h*   h*h*

Rafrivole
Rafrivole

Rafrivole
Rafrivole

....

16   Slanted romans   17   Mechanically-generated italics

only useful characteristic for producing differentiation. This view was held for a while and there was renewed interest in it again during the 1960s for photo-typesetting.[15] In our daily routines, we use them all the time, thanks to their prevalence in desktop publishing applications – but in typography, they are considered second-rate.

Even though seemingly different variants exist, there is usually just a single kind that gets a lot of use. When it comes to cursives, this is not surprising. There is only a problem concerning definitions. Already at the beginnings of their history, there was a great level of diversity. While searching for material on this subject, I came across an old writing manual from 1553. It is one of the earliest printed guidebooks about writing in the history of Northern European letterforms. It was published with the long title *Ein nutzlich und wolgegrundt Formular, Manncherlei schöner schriefften, Als Teuscher Lateinischer, Griechischer, vnnd Hebrayscher Buchstaben, sampt unterrichtung, wie ein jede gebraucht und lernen soll.* The author, Wolfgang Fugger, lived in Nuremberg from 1518 to 1558. He was a pupil of Johann Neudörffer, who was also an experienced writing master. His book describes the types of application for *chancery* handwriting styles systematically, assigning them to three different groups: *upright, left-leaning,* and *right-leaning.*[16]

The letterforms can, in turn, connect by different methods; Fugger mentions pointed, winding, arched and unconnected styles of writing. The scribe was free to pick and choose, which led to various hybrid forms *(bastards).* The author explained that 'everyone may learn what he wants and what he likes most' *(»mag ein jeder lernen welche er will vnd ime am basten gefelt«)*. Fugger's clear invitation proves that he did not believe there was a definitive way that cursive letters should look. It was only the writing direction that always remained constant – it ran from left to right.

In the middle of the 16th century, cursive styles with a humanistic character were being used south of the Alps, but there does not seem to have been any consensus regarding their forms among the writing masters there. For instance, the famous writing master Arrighi wrote in a cursive style that was almost upright.[17] On the other hand, his contemporary Giovannantonio Tagliente used a more free-form writing style.[18]

Tagliente's style does not come across as being arbitrary, but it is still very free-form. His left-leaning cursive has even more extreme traits than those of Fugger's. The writing masters maintained their freedom – there were no overarching conventions, as there had been with the Gothic *textura* and *rotunda* writing styles, for instance.[19] What has changed, then, in comparison with today? Actually not very much.

Perhaps the italic is defined today by its typographical function, meaning that it denotes something *special* in a text. Walter Tracy offers a sensible alternative, in which the term *style* would be more appropriate.[20] What defines this *style* – according to Tracy – is a topic I examine in the next chapter:

word → slant → *(connected)* → *italic style*

Although I am aware of the danger a superficial description presents, I think it makes sense to combine the existing terms. Whether written or printed – the italics always correspond to the same style of letterform. Not least to avoid confusion, I define this one term in this book:

italic

30

18 {↑} Detail from the *Formular* by Wolfgang
Fugger showing upright, slanted, winding
and woven writing styles. Nuremberg 1558

19 {F.} Spread from Giovannantonio Tagliente's
writing manual, which even contains a left-
leaning cursive. Venice 1515

Questa altra sorte di lettera benignissimo lettore se
adimanda lettera cancellaresca nodaresca per
essere per la sua grande dependentia corrente,
et si tira con le medesime regule e ragioni de
le ante scritte tabelle; la quale tu impararai
fare, sicome tu uedi qui in questa mostra
con li ammaistramenti li quali procedendo
intenderai.

et

per

maggiore

tua dilucidatione

io te scriuo lo sotto scritto alphabeto et
operando li nostri precetti ti farai bono scrittor

A aa. bb. cc. dd. ee. f ff. gg. hh. ij k. ll. m
mm. nn. oo pp. go. rr. ss. st t. u. uuy. y y.
.zz. & &.

Auenga che questa lettera sia pendente in
contrario dela ante scritta, et che la non sia in
consuetudine ad usar la uiuente di meno egli ha pu=
re de honore, et gloria a chi uora aprendo fare che
le altre a sapere fare anchor quella, non per bi=
sogno ma per suo diletto, atento che le cose narrate

sempre
sono
molto

agrate
alla natura nostra la quale lettera
a uoler la imparare, osserua
la regula dela ante
scritta et fa la
pendere
incontrario

. a. b. c. d. e. f. g. h. i. k. l. m. n. o. p. q. r. s. t. u. w.
x. y. z. & .

F

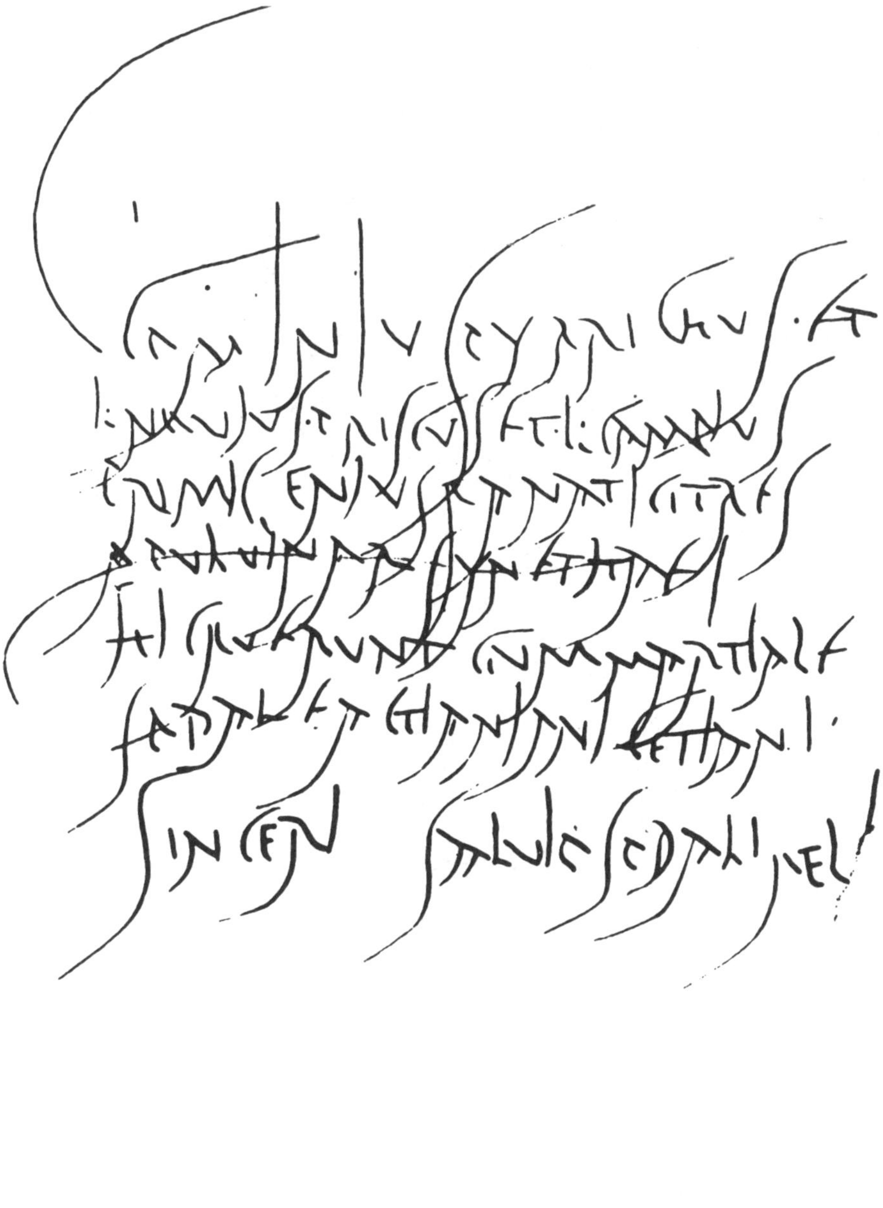

The history of the cursive style

The writing surrounding us day in and day out has undergone a long period of development where the letters were exposed to fashionable influences as well as to practical or technically-motivated ones. This part of the book attempts to reconstruct those changes as they apply to cursives or italics.

'Writing efficiency' played a major role for the cursive models that were implemented first. Their uninterrupted – or rather *fluid* – writing manner significantly enabled the copying of texts. The first humanistically-formed cursives were driven by efforts to speed up their execution. These were decisive for the development of typefaces familiar to us today.[21] Under certain circumstances, even casual writing can produce cursive features. For that reason, it seems sensible to summarise the historical changes since writing with the Latin script began – i.e., from the 3rd century B.C. onward.

It should also be noted that cursive's fate is closely linked to technical developments. These initially contributed to its spread, but also to its decline later. During their so-called *typographic naturalisation,* forms that had originated from the pen were transferred over to letterpress printing.* Since then, calligraphers and printers alike determined what proportions the script would have in equal measure. As a result of the adjustments made for printing, key characteristics were adopted that still determine the appearance of italics today. In addition to calligraphy, further possibilities for type design are now offered by PCs and Macintosh computers. The section 'Writing and printing' recounts how these simultaneous developments began.

The 'Refining the writing ductus' section reveals the interesting turning point where writing and printing were driven to almost fanatic extremes. This book's second part then concludes with a section called 'Developments through the present day'. Ultimately, the main focus on the emerging critical debate with historical cursives can be seen here.

One note seems necessary for me to add: since 95 per cent of a cursive's appearance is determined by lower-case letters, I will focus here on that 'small' part of the alphabet in particular.

20 Example of an early Roman cursive from about 300 B.C., which would have been used for everyday purposes. Often, texts like these were inscribed into wax tablets with a stylus.

*When punchcutters took up the roman minuscule for the first time, the letterforms already had a long history to look back on. Meanwhile, the italic's construction came from styles, and would even go on to inspire writing practices.

....

The origins of writing in Europe

The standardisation of the writing and reading directions were essential for the development of writeable characters. In the early 6th century B.C., people in southern Europe wrote from right to left at first. This was followed by writing in the boustrophedon style (which alternated between right-to-left and left-to-right), until finally in the 2nd century B.C. the method of writing from left to right asserted itself across the European regions.[22] The conditions under which writing was physically carried out contributed to the alphabet's gradually freeing itself from symmetry and positioning itself in a right-facing direction. Beginning in the 3rd century A.D., ascenders and descenders began to be added. These provided the basis for the first 'lower-case' or minuscule letters, like the *half-uncial* style.

The most important stage in the history of western writing was the development of the *Carolina,* or *Carolingian minuscule,* which appeared in Central Europe during the 9th century. It was characterized by previously-unachieved clarity and readability, thanks to its distinct ascenders and descenders. Additionally, its regular letter-spacing (rhythm) contributed to it giving a solid overall image to blocks of text. Uniform word spacing influenced the reading habit in such a way that one no longer read letter-by-letter, but rather in whole word images. [23] From the 9th through the 12th centuries, the *Carolina* was the dominant writing style for books and charters across the Western European cultural sphere. Although its genesis is closely linked with the intended reforms of the emperor Charlemagne (748 – 814), it is still unknown to what extent he contributed to its development himself.[24] Charlemagne's closest advisor, Alcuin of York (735–804), was commissioned to reform the educational system; on the one hand, he sought to remove the proliferation of errors in ecclesiastic and liturgical texts. On the other hand, his reforms centralised power within Charlemagne's enormous empire better. A result was that handwriting became standardised and this was the moment when the Latin lower-case letters were born.

right to left, 600 B.C.   boustrophedon, 500 B.C.   left to right, 400 B.C.

Construction differences resulting from various writing influences.

Capitalis and early minuscule, as they were used in Italy before the year 500.

Carolingian minuscule from the Alcuin's Vulgate Bible, 9th century. These letters are based on a four-lined system, since their bodies referenced a *baseline* and an *x-height,* as well as *ascenders* and *descenders.*

FENGVLA

Fençula

fengulam

noctis singula

About two hundred years after the disappearance of the *Carolingian minuscule,* the letterforms experienced a 15th-century revival. The Italian humanists were the driving influence here since they recognised their harmonious idea of man as having been realised in antiquity and now wanted to rekindle it. Therefore, they dedicated themselves to classical works, which they glorified as the pinnacle of human learning.[25] The humanists discovered a large number of manuscripts containing the works of Greek and Latin authors written with the above-mentioned *Carolingian minuscule.* Assuming that they had found manuscripts written in classical handwriting styles, humanist scribes adopted those exact forms into their repertoire, just as accurately as they had already adopted the epigraphic inscriptional capitals of Imperial Rome.

On the initiative of the poet Francesco Petrarca (1304–1374, also known as Petrarch), Coluccio Salutati (1331–1406) – who was then Chancellor of Florence – first began to integrate *late-Carolingian minuscule* forms into his gothic-style handwriting.[26]

Manuscripts written around 1400 by his pupil Poggio Braccioloni (1380–1459) – who was a secretary to Pope Boniface IX – are easily recognisable as being replicas of handwriting styles from the 10th and 11th centuries. Using these as a base, a handwriting style began to form that would later lead to the popular 15th century book-writing hand: the *Littera Antiqua.*[27]

Around the same time, Poggio's friend Niccolò Niccoli (1363–1437), who was also a pupil of Salutati, was developing a writing principle that was also based on the *Carolingian minuscule.* Yet because of the changes he incorporated, its flexibility – in terms of practicability – increased many times over. The first uses of these cursives can be found from 1420 onwards.[28] A closer look at these texts reveals a lighter image; the letterforms seem liberated and flow into one another. Due to a higher writing speed, a harmonious relationship between rhythm and dynamics had been developed. Moreover, diagonal connections were added in and between the letters – a result of the faster sideways-

{↖} Detail of a
humanist cursive,
1530

{→} A distinctly
humanist cursive
by the writing master
Hadrianus, 1490

.a.
Innocentius .iiͤ.
de elec. c.
venerabilem.

.b.
Gelasius. pp. xv.
q. vi. c. alius.

de senten. et rē
in. c. y. h. vi.

in suis scriptis ostendit q̃ aurum non tam
pretiosius sit plumbo q̃ regia potestate sit
altior ordo sacerdotalis. Stephanus q̃q:
papa secundus Romanum imperium
in personam magnifici Caroli a Grecis
transtulit in Germanos. Alius itē Ro
manus Pontifex Zacharias scilicet
Regem Francorum non tam pro suis in
iquitatibus q̃ pro eo quod tantę potestati
erat inutilis a regno deposuit: et Pipi
num Caroli magni imperatoris patrem
in eius locum substituit: omnesq: Fran
cigenas a iuramento fidelitatis absoluit.
Innocentius papa quartus Fridericum
Imperatorem suis ligatum peccatis &

movement of the pen. These connecting strokes were definitely no innovation; they were already being used in blackletter. Applied to the *Carolingian minuscule,* the development up to the *Cancellaresca* seems predictable.

Niccoli's contacts reached as far as Cosimo de' Medici (called the father of the fatherland), the real founder of the Medici glory. Niccoli was considered a perfectionist and a bibliophile antiquities collector, a friend of scholars, a stimulant for young people and a promoter of book-copying workshops. [29] In early-15th-century Florence, for instance, he set up a writing school that focused on teaching the humanistic cursive especially. His writing style made him very popular, and his reputation grew alongside his number of students. [30] According to Stanley Morison, Niccoli contributed more to the italic's development than any other contemporary competitors, as a result of these activities. Berthold Wolpe also described Niccoli as 'perhaps the first writer of the Italic'. [31]

This new cursive, which had the advantage of being clear in text and could also be written more quickly, was soon used in literary and diplomatic circles. During the pontificate of Eugene IV (1431–1447), it was adopted in the Papal Chancellery as the handwriting style for Papal briefs. [32] This resulted in its wide-reaching distribution across large parts of Europe.

Typographic naturalisation

At the beginning of the 15th century, the city of Venice could expand its supremacy in the field of printing. Their position was partly thanks to the merits of Teobaldo Manucci, who initially called himself Aldo Manuzio and later Latinised his name to Aldus Manutius (1450–1515). [33] He studied Latin in Rome and Greek in Ferrara, where he later held lectures of his own.

In addition to his teaching activities, Manutius had the idea of compiling all the surviving ancient Greek works together and publishing them at modest prices. Yet for this idea to work, he first had to find financing.

One of his students (Pico della Mirandola) recruited him as a tutor for his two nephews from the family of Prince Pio da Carpi. We know that Manutius later became very close to this family and that the Princess provided the financial support for his ambitious project. In 1488, when he was about forty years old, Manutius established a printing office in Venice, which was a city where both the wealthy customers for his books lived and where enough Greek immigrants – who would be able to carry out the necessary revisions

SANCTA CATHARINA DE SENIS.

26 The introduction of printed italics opened a new chapter in the history of letters. The illustration above reproduces the title page from a letter of St. Catherine of Siena, published in 1500.[34] It showcases the first known italics printed using movable metal type. About a year later, italic would be used as a book typeface for the first time.

Quia noueram mores hominum ; tum
etiam pertentare te prorsus uolui , q̃ recte
ista sentires. Sed omittamus haec iam tan
dem filĩ ; atq; ad eam partem sermonis,
ex qua egressi sumus, reuertamur.
B.   F.   Immo uero pater nec reuertamur: quid enim amplius nobiscum pla
tanis illis? de iis enim loquebamur.
Sed (si placet)ad Aetnam potius, de qua
sermo haberi coeptus est , properemus.
B.   P.   • Mihi uero pérplacet;
ita tamen , ut ne festines: tibi enim ego
omnes has pomeridianas horas dico.
Sed quoniam me impellente nimium
iam extra Aetnae terminos prouecti su
mus, non cõmittam , ut te interpellem
saepius ; nisi quid erit , quod de ea ipsa te
rogem.   B.   F.   Sanè mons ip
se situ, forma, magnitudine, feritate, in-
cendiis mirus; demum tota sui qualitate
ac specie longe conspicuus, et sibi uni par
est. Ab aurora mare Ionium bibit; et Ca

and corrections to the collected manuscripts – were gathered. In his house near the church of Sant' Agostino, many Greek scholars were busy editing the collected manuscripts, while Manutius himself was reproducing them, thanks to the help of a group of talented typographers.* He learned the craft of printing from his later father-in-law, Andreas Torresanus of Asola. The latter came into the possession of Nicolas Jenson's printing office and typographic materials in 1479. Manutius began to work with exactly those typefaces.[35] However, the main work of creating the characters (from the year 1490 onward) was carried out by the skilled punchcutter Francesco da Bologna, called Griffo.

Initially, only Greek (and later Roman) classics were printed, mostly in large editions. Each title page was decorated with the same signet: an anchor with a dolphin. This symbolized speed and consistency and became a hallmark for scholarly quality. It stood above the motto was *Festina lente,* meaning 'make haste slowly'.[36]

After several publications succeeded on the market – including Pietro Bembo's treatise *De Aetna,* printed in 1495/96, and the *Hypnerotomachia Poliphili* (1499), which were each composed with further-developments of roman type called *Poliphilus* – Manutius achieved a commercial breakthrough by introducing the small-octave book format (142.5 × 225 mm).

Known as *Aldines,* these forerunners of today's paperbacks, had significant advantages over the *Folio* format (210 × 330 mm) that was common at the time: they allowed a printer to increase his capacity while also cutting costs. The books offered previously-unknown ease-of-use for readers, as they now could fit comfortably inside a pocket.[37] Their lower sale-price – also a result of their smaller size – contributed to their popularity, too. Composition with a particularly narrow printing type was an important part of the production of *Aldines.* This led to the first use of italic type, in an edition of Virgil from 1501. With this type it was possible to fit up to fifty characters with a body size of 10.7 Didot points onto a line measuring only 6.8 cm.[38] Additionally, there were a considerable number of ligatures: more than sixty ligatures can be counted, which were based on handwritten models.[39] In this way, both economic and technical circumstances contributed to the integration of italics into typography.

In the further development of roman type, printers usually referenced handwritten *humanistic minuscules.* Griffo most likely had handwritten cursive alphabets at his disposal, too.[40] According to legend, the letterforms he cut were based on manuscripts from Petrarch, but a more realistic hypothesis

*Aldus Manutius published works from Bembo, Erasmus, …saeus, Hesiod, Terence, Theocritus, Theognis, ·istophanes, Herodotus, Thucydides, Sophocles, Seneca, Euripides, ·emosthenes, Aeschylus, Lysis, Plato, Plautus, Pindar, Plutarch, Quintilian and others. ·n doing so, he not only contributed to the ·/elopment of the italics also to the rediscovery of antiquity during the Renaissance.

The signet used in books from Aldus Manutius' publishing house, 1495–1515

{↖} Pietro Bembo's *De Aetna* treatise, 1495/96

is that they are a variation of the *Cancellaresca* developed on the model of Arrighi's handwriting. Griffo might also have been their originator himself. He was a multi-talented artisan who was well-versed in calligraphy.[41] Yet the real identity of the handwritten sources he relied on remains a mystery.

The new pocketbooks became a cultural and commercially important export article, primarily because of the relatively high number of copies printed, as well as the novelty of the books' size.* Manutius' printing office was therefore able to stay dominant in Europe until after his death in 1515.

However, competitors in Italy, France and Germany were alert and unabashedly copied the editions that Manutius had invested so much time and money in.[42] This ensured that the Venetian italic became widespread across Europe. The Italian *incunabula* spurred French printers to imitate cursive typefaces, which were then called *Italique*.

The Manutian design principle remained unchanged into the 16th century and was then further optimized.[43] Manutius' fundamental idea of using italics for space-saving reasons, however, was rarely pursued by later printers.

At the same time, the upright roman was being developed, which later replaced italics as the primary typeface for text. This process was slow to set in, however, and was the result of the intentions of French printers. The Manutius family reprinted the *Aldines* long after Manutius' death in 1515. Their printing office finally closed down in 1597, after his grandson died. The development of the first italic capital letters was initially a slow process. The letters of the Roman majuscule alphabets had just been rediscovered by the Italian humanists and were only of minor interest for the italic's overall development.

*Gustav Stresow wrote in his 1993 article on italics that *'the choice of italics is to be attributed to the idealistic intentions [of Aldus] because with them he imposed considerable additional burdens on typeface production and typesetting'. Stresow added that 'Aldus' punch-cutters and typefounders had already managed to overcome these difficulties, however, since the Greek types his printing office used were also slanted.'* Quoted from: Antiquariat, Issue 2, 1993 (Supplement to the Börsenblatt für den Buchhandel)[44]

29 Closeup of the *Aldine italic* showing the ligatures for no/cti/si/gu, 1500

30 {→} Aldus' Virgil edition in a small-octave format, 1501

tanam suftinet imo in pede : cum sole
descendit in insulam_ ,qua Tyrrenum
pelagus est ;et quae Aeoliæ appellantur:
laterorsus , in sept...
Pelorus obiicitur...
sunt : contra reliq...
ctúsque iiomnes ,...
Africam protend...
dices suas ferè in o...
cubi orientem , et...
misso cliuo pauli...
degit ; et nullius n...
gium caste intra f...
tur . circumitur n...
pass. ascenditur fe...
uior uia_. Imi col...
ambitus per opp...
quens inhabitatu...
Cerere feraces te...
mnis generis supr...
Hic amoeniffima...
fluuii personante...

I psa sub ora uiri cœlo uenêre uolantes,
E t uiridi federe folo,tum maximus heros
M aternas agnofcit aues,Lætus'q; precatur.
E fte duces,o fiqua uia eft,curfum'q; per auras
D irigite in lucos,ubi pinguem diues opacat
R amus humum,tu'q;o dubiis ne defice rebus
A lma parens.Sic effatus ueftigia preffit,
O bferuans quæ figna ferant,quo tendere pergant
P afcentes,illæ tantum prodire uolando,
Q uantum acie poffent oculi feruare fequentum.
I nde ubi uenere ad fauces graue olentis Auerni,
T ollunt fe celeres,liquidum'q; per aera lapfæ,
S edibus optatis gemina fuper arbore fidunt,
D ifcolor unde auri per ramos aura refulfit.
Q uale folet fyluis brumali frigore uifcum
F ronde uirere noua,quod non fua feminat arbos,
E t croceo fœtu teretes circundare truncos,
T alis erat fpecies auri frondentis opaca
I lice,fic leni crepitabat bractea uento.
C orripit extemplo Aeneas,auidus'q; refringit
C unctantem,et uatis portat fub tecta Sibyllæ,
N ec minus interea Mifenum in littore Teucri
F lebant,et cineri ingrato fuprema ferebant.
P rincipio pinguem tedis,et robore fecto
I ngentem ftruxere pyram,cui frondibus atris
I ntexunt latera,et ferales ante cupreffos
C onftituunt,decorant'q; fuper fulgentibus armis
P ars calidos latices,et ahena undantia flammis
E xpediunt,corpus'q; lauant frigentis,et ungunt
F it gemitus,tum membra toro defleta reponunt,

In general, three kinds of upper-case letters emerged during the Renaissance. A first version was derived from the study of *Carolingian* manuscripts. Another model integrated capitals from the Romans. The third variant was characterized by the use of so-called *swash* capitals. These were a reaction to the use of hammers and chisels, since they integrated calligraphic components into their forms. Their application was context-specific; they were used more often in texts than in headings, for instance.[45]

It was customary in calligraphic circles to use upright capitals, even in hastily written compositions. Looking at the writing models of the old masters, it is clear that they treated capital letters with respect. Statements by the writing master Arrighi confirm that he thought capitals should be written 'in a firm, trusting manner, and without inner trembling', so that they 'do not lose their gracefulness and lightness'.[46] Printers incorporated this knowledge into their punchcutting.

A closer look at the basic differences to the lower-case letters reveals that the preferred embedding of upright capitals into cursive bodies of text has a certain logic. Like numerals, capital letters are an independent group, subject to laws of their own. Classical forms' construction originated in the directionless writing practised by the Greeks and the Romans. The symmetrical letters had to be grasped by the eye in both reading directions. On the other hand, italics had their own rules: their natural dynamic ideal tended toward a single direction.

{←} Ornamented
initial letter from
a chapter opening.
G. A. Castiglione,
Milan 1557

2 {↗} Upright
lower-case cursive
letters adapted to
the capitals, 1528

Nter omnia liberalium artium maximaꝗ̃ꝗ̃
doctrinarum genera, eas disciplinas, ceteris
omnibus præstare putamus. quæ ueritate̅,
facilius inuenire, et inuentam poſſunt uberi-
ori quadam et rerum et sententiarum copia
declarare, Nam, cum uniuscuiusꝗ̃ scientiæ, ꝑ
sapienter quidem pro fine, constituiſſet. Cũ
d illum propius acceſſerit, eam, cœteris omni-
rtibus, præstare putauerunt. Et guanꝗ̃ om-
guodam societatis uinculo contineantur. dispa-
nter se. Vnaꝗ̃ inter illas, maxime excellit. gue-
ꝛe primæ ueritatis, et eius cognitione uersatur
logia appellatur. Nam, alia disciplinæ, atgue
guandam ueritatis, proſpiciunt. hæc autem
, nobis clariſſima guadãm suce sua commo-
ꝗ̃ plurimæ partes in ea contineantur. quæ ꝑ
ſſime præstent. Nihil tamen post admirabile̅,
per Moysem promulgatam, et post sanctiſſima
iosius, atgꝫ facilius. ꝗ̃ Epistolas Pauli, prestare
s. Nam, cum illæ, clariſſimum guendam ſplen-
onem ueritatis, nobis afferant. guæ, in illa ꝑ
Moysi, sub uelamentis figurarum, latitare
modo ueterem illam legem euangelicæ uerita
t, atgꝫ utranꝗ̃, unam fœcerunt, sed omnium
um improbos ausus. nephariosꝗ̃ eorum cogita-

While calligraphers manually compensated for the interplay between both letter styles, more drastic steps were necessary for letterpress printing. The production of metal italic types provided a supporting reason for cleaning up the shaky coexistence between the dynamic lower-case letters and the static upper-case.

Even with Manutius, a distant relationship between upper-case and lower-case letters is still visible because of the generous spacing between them. After all, the italic capitals were produced so that they were about a third smaller than the ascenders and descenders, in order to not outshine the lower-case letters.[47]

Adding in-strokes, flourishes and tails to various *swash capitals* was an important step, at least in calligraphic circles, toward bringing some calligraphic facets into the italic. This also led to the use of alternate decorative letters. Some printers dispensed with the slanted nature of the lower-case letters altogether so that these would harmonise better with the capitals, but in doing so they removed the italics' most distinctive characteristic.

In the end, almost forty years went before capital letters were developed that could be viewed as being italic today. The *Basel Italic* used by the printer Johann Froben (1460 – 1527) in Basel from 1518 and by the printer Sebastian Gryphius (1492 – 1556) in Lyon 1527/28, is an exception; its capitals are slanted.[48]

Concrete steps in developing the typical slant only began when it became more common to forcibly mix italics with roman. In that situation, it was necessary to make the upper-case and lower-case letters of both styles distinguishable from one another. The interplay of both styles thus accelerated the italicisation of capital letters. The more that mixing occurred in a text, the greater the number of slanted capitals would be.

{←} Swash capitals
from a humanist
scribe

{→} The first slanted
capitals, from the
Basel Italic by Johann
Froben, 1528

LIBER

Cui licet accedat *V*irtus, tamen usque priores
Fert Fatum parteis in re quacunque gerenda.
   Fato Romani post tot discrimina, post tot
Prælia, debellatum Orbem rexere monarchæ:
Roma caputq; fuit Mundi, priùs exiguus grex
Quam pastorum habitabat, & errans exul ab aruis
Finitimis (ut asylum) post scelus omne colebat.
Mox Fato inclinante, suis spoliata triumphis
Corruit, & patrio (infandum) iugulata tyranno
Nil, nisi nomen, habet Romæ, desertaq; sordet.
   Fato etiam Græci nil non potuere uel armis,
*V*el studiis:terra omni posthabita, auxit *A*thenas

Writing and printing

The introduction of printing presses caused an unprecedented decline for a writing tradition that had lasted over more than a thousand years. The complexer that books became, the less often they were written out by hand.[49] However, as the *scriptoria* progressively declined in the middle of the 15th century, the writing-master profession was gradually being established – a deviation from the trend mentioned above.* This new profession was closely linked to the expansion of bourgeois school systems and it continued into the 19th century.

Evidence for this is preserved in the many writing books. Even though these were first written on paper, they were then cut by experienced engravers (either as a negative or as a positive in long-grain wood) and printed in smaller book formats. From this movement, writing by hand would develop over the next two to three hundred years into an distinguished and widespread discipline. The fact that the documents of the writing masters often fell into the hands of printers, who used them as a source of inspiration for their own book types, encouraged calligraphers to refine the Humanist italics even further. The popularity of the style increased continuously, not least due to the countless manuscripts from renowned Italian calligraphers like Hippolytus, Marco, Vicenza or Paudua. The Humanistic cursive became the favoured handwriting style among scholars, artists and kings. For example, the correspondence of both King Edward IV and Queen Elisabeth I were in Humanistic-style handwriting.[50] Benvenuto Cellini and Michelangelo each wrote Humanistic cursive in quick and artistic hands. To this day, traditional italics are still based on this Humanistic system of writing.

The Italian writing masters themselves called this cursive style *Cancellaresca.* At the beginning of the 16th century, its use was divided into two basic variants: the elegant *Cancellaresca Corsiva* featured visually-striking flourishes on the ascenders and descenders. The *Cancellaresca Formata,* however, was a separate variant written with much shorter, serif-like terminals on ascenders, instead of flourishes. At the same time, other variants existed whose styles depended on calligraphers' temperaments. Essentially, they were all written with a broad nib whose pen tip was rotated about 45 degrees relative to the baseline.

Of the Italian writing masters, Ludovico Vicentino (Arrighi), Giovannantonio Tagliente and Giambattista Palatino were among the best known. However, Arrighi probably achieved the greatest fame of all of them – perhaps because he was intensively involved with the adoption of his handwriting into print.

*The decline of the monastic writing system already began in the early 13th century. One of the reasons for this was the emergence of the first universities. They employed so-called lay stationer merchants, whose output replaced copies from the *scriptoria.* This example only represents a sketch; the causes of the decline can not be definitively delineated.

quella quella

35 Two variations on the *Cancellaresca,* handwritten by Ludovico Arrighi: *Formata,* around 1523 and *Corsiva,* around 1526

36 {↗} A letter to Michelangelo by the venturesome goldsmith Benvenuto Cellini, 1561

Eccellentissimo et molto mio osseruandissimo M Michelagnolo

Per ch'io nõ credo, ch mai altr'omo nascessi al mondo, piu affetionato
alle gran'uirtu ure di quello, ch sono stato io, cominciando
a cognoscerle quando io lauoraro della bella oreficeria
et p esser in uaghito di quelle ure uniche uirtu, nõ mi
pareua d'hauer satisfatto alla honesta uoglia mia, se pri=
ma io nõ uenino conessa alla mirabile sculturo, p̃ õ
sempre amandoui, et osseruandoui io mi son fatto qualche
honore et tutto di pende da uoi.

Hora considerato che gl homini ueramente sono obligati
d ad amare, et osseruar l'uno l'altro: trouandomi io
adunque un mio lauorate, il quale p le grã bõtã sua
mi son fatto compare, et uedutolo uolto, p alcuni sua
cõmodi, auenirsene in cotesta bella roma; ancora sapu
to da lui et altre uolte egli ui ha seruito in nel fare
certi capitelli p la grã fabbrica di S. Pietro: doue io
son certissimo p esser lui homo ualete nel arte, et hij
ui debbe essere riuscito: p̃ la prego, et p amor mio ui
ui degniate di metterlo Topa ch'io uene terro molta obli=
gatione: et gondoui sempre ch mi comãdiate: et Jddio
felicissimo lungamente mi conserui. Di Firẽ il di 9 di settem
bre 1561   seruitore parutissimo alli comandi uostri

Benuenuto Cellini

He was not only a professional calligrapher and the scribe for apostolic briefs, but also a publisher, teacher, printer and type designer.[51]

Arrighi was from Vincenza. After contributing to the publication of a travel book, he devoted himself to calligraphy between 1517 and 1520 in Venice. He then went on to Rome to work as a *scrittore de brevi apostolici* (Papal brief writer). Between 1522 and 1527, he printed small exquisite books there.[52]

La Operina is his first and probably most well-known publication, for this made it possible for non-specialists to learn the Humanistic cursive, too. Neither Arrighi himself nor his bookseller put profitable interests in the foreground; rather, it was Arrighi's intention to meet the constant requests of his admirers for handwritten study-alphabets in a labour-saving way.

His important debut feature by no means consisted of handwritten originals. His calligraphy was cut into wood by the block-cutter Ugo da Carpi. The extent to which this influenced the authenticity of Arrighi's letterforms remains unclear to this day.

Paul Standard – a student of the famous calligrapher Edward Johnston – made the very stimulating book, *Arrighi's Running Hand: A Study of Chancery Cursive,* which was published in New York in 1979. It deals with Arrighi's theories and also contains a complete translation of the *Operina.* Careful analyses of the handling of the broad pen make it possible to still write the Humanistic cursive today, using this original.[53]

The simplicity of *La Operina* as a booklet is surprising. Over the course of 32 very clearly designed pages – consisting of a 16-page introduction and 16 writing samples – the same handwriting guides the reader through the booklet in a friendly tone and with precise clarity.

Arrighi's theory begins with two different strokes. Each lower-case letter should begin with one of them: either a short, thick stroke or a long, thin slash. Since the shape of each character should be narrow and slanted rather than round and upright, each letter is fitted into an upright parallelogram. A total of 18 letters can be written in a single stroke, i.e., without the pen being set down; all others are written with two strokes.

Other possible variations are listed consecutively. Rules for letter and word spacing rounded out the instructions. Arrighi preferred to place his majuscules vertically, with their exact forms adapted to a word's structure and dependent on context. Furthermore, lines should be spaced sufficiently enough that ascenders and descenders would not touch each other.

*Cut by the goldsmith Lautizio Perugino, who was Arrighi's business partner until 1525.

A second book printed in Vincenza in 1523 with the title *Il modo de temperare le penne,* contained Arrighi's first italic printing typeface.* The formal character of the letters is strongly based on those in the writing manual *La Operina.*

Seguita lo essempio delle' lre' che pono
ligarsi con tutte'le' sue sequenti, in tal me
do cioe'

aa ab ac ad ae' af ag ah ai ak al am an

ao ap aq ar as af at au ax ay az

Il medesmo farai con d i k l m n u.

Le ligature' poi de' c f s ʃ t ʃomo

le' infra =

scritte

et, fa ff fi fm fn fo fr fu fy,
ʃt ʃt

ʃf ʃʃ ʃʃ ʃt, ta te' ti tm tn to tg tr tt tu

tx ty

Con le restanti' littere' de lo Alphabeto, che'
ʃono, b e' g h o p q r x y z z

non si deue' ligar mai lra

alcuna sequente'

Over the following three years, Arrighi continued to develop two more italic typefaces, which only differed in a few details. For instance, there is variation in the nature of the ascenders, out-strokes and tails. In 1524, a difference between *u* and *v* was introduced into these italics for the first time. Regarding the typefaces, Stanley Morison hypothesised that they might either be the same typeface or gradations of an ongoing development process.[54] Concerning Arrighi's motivation, Morison ruled out that he was working toward the offering of low-cost editions of the classics, like Manutius. Instead, he must have been driven by an interest in beauty and beautiful forms.[55]

There is much less information about the printer/writing master Giovannantonio Tagliente than about Arrighi. In a note on Giovannantonio Tagliente, James Wardrop reproduced a petition to the Doge of Venice and the Venetian Republic's Great Council (c. 1491). This had been written by Tagliente in a *Cancellaresca* that was extraordinary, due to its rhythmic elegance and precise style. In this petition, Tagliente requested a scholarship that would allow him to stay in the city. In return, he promised to teach the *Cancellaresca* to the young servants in the Doge's chancellory. Although his request was denied, the next year saw Tagliente already working as a seneschal (servant of the court) at the *Fondaco dei Tedeschi* on the Grand Canal, next to the Rialto bridge.[56]

Today, Tagliente's idiosyncratic style seems liberated. This is evident, among other things, from the rather impartial approach he took with the numerous flourishes or the very soft forms. The fact that Tagliente followed developments in arts and crafts with great interest and felt inspired by them could be an explanation for this.* In 1524, he decided to follow the trend and produce a writing manual. Entitled the *Opera che insegna a scrivere,* this was published in Venice. The block-cutter Eustachio Celebrino copied Tagliente's handwritten originals onto wooden blocks. His son Pietro was also involved in the production. The book contains numerous *merchantescha* (merchant scripts) and other handwriting styles. The great number of different alphabets testify to Tagliente's remarkable teaching experience. The book was extremely successful and was reprinted at least thirty times.

*A. S. Osley wrote about Tagliente that 'he loved the bold shapes, the ornamental stroke of the nib. Some have criticised his boasting and exuberance, but no one can doubt his vitality.'[57]

Le litere cancellaresch e sono molto a orate a grandi honoxi,

Da altri, quando sono fatte con mesura, & arte, e tanto

piuj sono aorde quando es la litera e a com pagnata co

qualche gagliardo Trato. si come Tu uedi qui. voledola

imparare obserua li sequenti nostri precetti tenendo lo

soto scritto alphabeto p tuo esemplo et g Imparerai a

tirar

li ditti

trati aduno p uno cun la g yeloce & iuiuace tua

mano & praticado Ti farai suficiete

a .aa. bb. cc. dd. e. ff. g g.

i ij. k. ll. l l. a ss. m m. n n. oo. pp. q q.

q. rr. ss ß ſ t. u u. r. xx. y y. z & G

D

De' sopradetti tre' Tratti, siano false', ò
uero imaginatiue', & non
cauate' dalla esperientia
geometricamente';
per
esser' impossibile' misurare'
effettualmente' vna cosa si piccola, hò
voluto aprire' il modo ritrouato da me',
co'l quale' hò visto chiara
mente' esser
cosi.
Et però, uolendo uenire' alla prat
tica, & uedere' per esperien
tia le' sopradette' misure',
potrete' pigliare'
vna

The third in the group of 16th-century writing masters was Giambattista Palatino, born in Rossano (Calabria). He worked as a secretary at the Accademia dei Sdegnati in Rome, where – as a prominent citizen – he frequented intellectual circles.

Palatino was also an exceptionally gifted calligrapher. His 1524 book, *Libro nel Qual s'ingna a scrivere,* has a large collection of multi-faceted alphabets, some of which Alfred Fairbank described as 'curiosities'. The most important peculiarities of his writing method, however, can only be seen in the details, because the structure of his *Cancellaresca* did not change at first. Like Arrighi, he placed his letters into very narrow, oblique parallelogram-shaped spaces, and their forms were twice as high as they were wide.[58] His very stringent, almost mechanical approach was characteristic. The lowercase letters were composed of the three basic directions: horizontal *(testa),* vertical *(traverso)* and diagonal *(taglio).* From time to time Palatino's *Cancellaresca* seems to have slightly exaggerated pointed ridges that look almost Gothic. However, this did not prevent Hermann Zapf from using it as the basis for his *Palatino* typeface.

Palatino's instructions are comprehensive and extremely stimulating. An interesting example is his special method for achieving calligraphic ability, which Palatino practiced himself and with his students. According to this, the sample alphabets were first engraved into either hardwood or copper and then traced with a *stylus.* Later, one would practice writing between four guidelines for several days, then on just one line and finally without any help.[59]

{P. 47} Page from *La Operina* by Ludovico Vicentino (Arrighi), 1522

{P. 49} Page from the *Lo presente libro Insegna,* 2nd edition, by Giovannantonio Tagliente, 1524

{←} *Libro nel Qual s'insigna a scrivere* by Giambattista Palatino, 1528

As the writing books of the 16th century show, European letter styles gradually evolved along two important strands. One direction grew out of Humanistic cursives, the other out of Gothic letterforms. Both emerging directions were variations brought about by writing with a broad nib, which is why hybrid letterforms were more common in the calligraphic sector than in typography. However, out of the great variety in letterform styles that were then being used, hybrids were seldom.[60] You can find rare examples in Wolfgang Fugger's *Formular*. The italics depicted there suggest a relationship to the *Fraktur* type. The so-called 'roman' typefaces – whose existence was increasingly determined by the participation of French master printers – remained unaffected by this.

Beginning in 1529, the centre of new typeface production gradually shifted to France. This period went down in history as the 'golden age of French typography', marked by publications from printers like Estienne, Geoffrey Tory, Simon de Colines, Jean de Tournes and Jacques Kerver.[61]

Taking inspiration from Italian *incunabula,* the first *Italiques* – whose Italian origins were clearly recognisable, just as in their in roman types – were developed in Lyon or Paris.

For instance, Simon de Colines worked in Paris from 1520 to 1546. When he used italics in his printing office for the first time, they included elements taken from Aldus Manutius' and Arrighi's designs.

{←} Variations on interrupted handwriting by Wolfgang Fugger, 1553

{→} First version of Arrighi's italic printing typeface, 1523

{↘} Simon de Coline's first italics (which have a clear affinity to their Italian predecessors), 1532

Dele uarie forti de littere poi, che in questo Tratta-
tello trouerai, se io ti uolessi ad una per una descriuere
tutte le sue ragioni, saria troppo longo processo ; Ma
tu hauendo uolunta de' imparare', ti terrai inanzi que
sti exempietti, et sforcerati imitarli quanto pote-
rai, che in ogni modo seguendo quelli, senon in tutto,
almeno in gran parte' te adiuterano conseguire quella
forte' di littera, che' piu in esso ti dilettera'. Piglialo

Nuenta secuit primus qui naue profundum,
Et rudibus remis sollicitauit aquas :
Qui dubijs ausus committere flatibus alnum:
Tranquillis primum trepidus se credidit vndis:
Littora securo tramite summa legens.
Mox longos tentare sinus, & linquere terras,
Et leni cœpit pandere vela noto.
Ast vbi paulatim præceps audacia creuit:
Cordáq3 languentem dedidicere metum:
Iam vagus irrupit pelago:cælúmq3 secutus,
Ægæas hyemes Ioniúmq3 domat.

The English bibliographer A. F. Johnson called the 16th century 'the Age of Italics', since especially in the Italian regions, whole books were printed in italic.[62] Elizabeth Eisenstein's book *The Printing Press as an Agent of Change* gives an interesting accoung of this.[63]

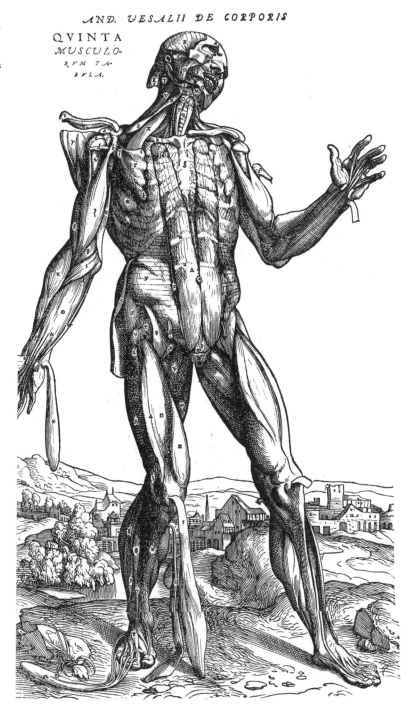

AND. UESALII DE CORPORIS

QVINTA
MUSCULO-
RVM TA-
BVLA.

HVMANI FABRICA LIBER II.

L Os υ imaginem referens, à quo primum & secundum & tertium par eorum qui id mouent musculorum resecuimus.

M Primus & secundus linguæ musculi ab osse υ referente pronati.

N Laryngis cartilago, scutum referens, & iam narrandis musculis adhuc obtecta.

O Dexter duorum musculorum, qui ab osse υ referente, in cartilaginem scuto similem inseruntur.

P Dexter duorum musculorum, qui à pectoris osse scutum imitanti laryngis cartilagini inseruntur. Ad huius musculi exterius latus, congeries uisitur soporariæ arteriæ, interioris uenæ iugularis, & sexti cerebri neruorum paris.

Q Asperæ arteriæ anterior sedes.

R,S Musculus ossi υ referenti proprius, & à scapulæ superiori costa enatus. Singuli characteres singulos ipsius indicant uentres. Pars autem in horum medio consistens, eius musculi sedes est, tendinis substantiæ non absimilis.

T Portio musculorum secundi paris caput mouentium.

V Tertius scapulam mouentium musculus, ex transuersis superiorum ceruicis uertebrarum processibus initium ducens.

X Quoniam hic locus nihil aliud peculiariter, quàm septima tabula in homine ostendisset: & quia in Galeni uerba iurati, ipsius sententiæ, quum hæc pingerentur, plus æquo fauimus: musculum hic ex cane delineatum cernis, quo homines prorsus destituuntur, & qui Galeno tertius thoracem mouentium habetur, sequenti tabula integer Γ notandus.

Y Dextri lateris clauiculam hic à pectoris osse auulsimus, adhuc summo humero connexam, & sibi adhuc musculum seruantem, qui thoracis motorum primus numerabitur, hicq̄ Z insignitur.

a Summus humerus, seu scapulæ elatior processus.

b Interior demissior ue scapulæ processus.

c Ligamentum brachy ossis ad scapulam articuli peculiarium quartum ab interiori scapulæ processu summum petens humerum.

d Ligamentum teres, ab apice interioris scapulæ processus, in anteriorem sedem externi capitis humeri insertum, ac huius articuli, post membraneum omnibus articulis commune, primum.

e Aliud teres ligamentum, ex eminentissima scapulæ acetabuli sede, ad externum quoq̄ humeri caput procedens, atq̄ huius articuli peculiarium ligamentorum secundum.

f Hac sede duo ligamenta, d & e insignita, suis lateribus uniuntur, & uelut transuersum efformant ligamentum, transmittens caput externum musculi cubitum flectentium anterioris, ac mox ʒ notandi.

g Pectoris os, cui septem superiorum costarum cartilagines utrinq̄ connectuntur.

h Prima thoracis costa: reliquæ dein etiam, unà cum ipsarum interuallis, citra characterum opem sunt cōspicuæ.

Γ Musculus scapulam mouentium primus. *i* & *k* huius musculi principium notant, quandam manus speciem

i,k,l. perinde in exortu, ac musculus ipsi succumbens, & *m* insignitus, in insertione repræsentans. *l* tendinem præsentis musculi indicat. Porro *i,k* & *l* simul, huius musculi trianguli speciem quodammodo ostendunt.

m Musculus, qui à scapulæ basi pronatus, octo superioribus thoracis costis inseritur.

Δ Dexter rectorum abdominis musculorum. Ac *n* carneum recti abdomini musculi principium, triangulo non

n,o. absimile notat. *o* principium eiusdem musculi nerueum inscribitur, penè uniuersum efformans musculum. To-

p,q. to interuallo, à *p* ad *q* pertinête, recti abdominis musculi internis suis lateribus cōtingunt. Tota autem sede supra *q*, aut mox supra umbilicum consistente, tanto magis musculi mutuo seiunguntur, quanto altius conscendunt. Cæterùm *q* notabit etiam obliquorum abdominis musculorum neruosæ tenuitatis, ad transuersim

r. abdominis musculum, hac in parte ad pectoris usq̄ sedem connexum. Porro *r* linea insignitur, quæ carneam recti musculi partem finit, quæq̄ ultima ipsius insertionis in homine est portio, uti in quarta tabula ad characte-

s. rem *n* est cernere. Intercapedine igitur ab *r* ad *s* pertinente, se offert recti simiæ abdominis musculi tendo seu

t. membrana, excarnis ue musculi pars. *t* autem indicat carneam musculi sedem, primæ costæ & secundæ thoracis insertam. est latus ille tendo & carnea hæc pars is musculus, quem Galenus quintum thoracæ mouentium enumerat, in hominibus haudquaquam, ut in caudatis simijs ❀nibus, conspicuus. Nos autem hic illum, Galenum intelligendi gratia, delineauimus, quòd alioquin hæc pectoris sedes, sequentium duarum tabularum pe-

u,u,u. ctoribus erat absq̄ huis musculiu responsura. Postremò, *u,u,u* notantur inscriptiones, seu neruea delineamenta, transuersim recto musculo impressa, quibus obliquè ascendentis musculi neruosa exilitas pertinacissimè connascitur.

x Linea hæc portiunculam notat musculi abdominis obliquè ascendentis, qua is transuerso abdominis musculo inibi adeò ualide committitur, ut inter dissecandum, nisi relicto eiusmodi signo, à transuerso liberari nequeat.

y Transuersus abdominis musculus.

α Obliquè ascendens abdominis musculus, ab abdomine hic reflexus.

β Vasorum

Claude Garamond also adopted the Italians' typefaces, which he only made minor changes to. Garamond's early designs have a lot in common with the romans from Francesco Griffo. Around 1540, Garamond's popularity increased considerably. This may have encouraged him to design future typefaces that were free from Italian influence, which in turn eventually established themselves as brands. Yet Garamond's fame did not come from producing Latin alphabets, but from the making the *Grec du Roi* instead, a bespoke Greek typeface for the French king. Although Garamond also designed an *Italique* based on Arrighi's model, his influence on italic development is considered insignificant.[64] Under her pseudonym Paul Beaujon, Beatrice Warde wrote in her detailed *Fleuron 5* article from 1926 that 'Garamont had so little interest in Italic that he copied the Aldine letter badly as a money-making scheme in 1545 and let it go at that'.[65]

Garamond's level of recognition today rests on a misunderstanding: another roman that appeared much later (around 1615) was accidentally attributed to Claude Garamond. However, its creator was not Claude Garamond from Paris, but Jean Jannon from Sedan. This momentous error lasted well into the 20th century. Large type foundries were already selling multiple revivals under the name 'Garamond'. By the time the error was noticed, Garamond was already synonymous with that later classic typeface style.[66]

Modern Garamond typefaces based on Claude Garamond's actual work, like *Adobe Garamond* from Robert Slimbach (published in 1989), have been supplemented with italics based on those of the French master Robert Granjon (1513–1589). Garamond's contemporary gave the italics quite a specific look. This makes him much more interesting for this chapter.

Granjon, the son of a Parisian printer, grew up in Lyon and began his career as a goldsmith before becoming a punchcutter in 1543. As a publisher, he brought out a Greek–Latin edition of the New Testament in 1549. Between 1545 and 1588, he received more commissions in Lyon, Antwerp, Paris and Rome. Although Granjon also knew how to produce roman types, it is obvious that his talent lay in making italic typefaces.[67] Stanley Morison, a typographic consultant to the Monotype Corporation, wrote that 'he is unquestionably the greatest master of Italics of his age'.[68]

Granjon had a close relationship with the printer and publisher Christoph Plantin in Antwerp. This led him to work alternately in Paris and Antwerp, where he cut roman types, several italics and a Greek typeface. Additionally, Christoph Plantin also commissioned a *Civilité* or a special kind of script-cursive. This was first used in the book *Dialogue de la Vie et la Mort* by Innocenzio Ringhieri, printed at Lyon. Its external form did not exactly correspond to the typical ideal for italics at that time. Nevertheless, Max Caflisch considers

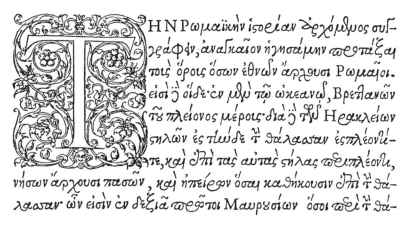

ΗΝ Ρωμαϊκὴν ἱστορίαν ἀρχόμβνος συγγράφψν, ἀναγκαῖον ἡγησάμην προταξαι τοῖς ὅροις ὅσων ἐθνῶν ἄρχουσι Ρωμαῖοι. εἰσὶ ὃ οἵδε ἐν μὲν τῷ ὠκεανῷ, Βρεπανῶν τῆ πλείονος μέρους διὰ ὃ τῶν Ἡρακλείων στηλῶν ἐς τῶδε τ θάλασαν ἐσπλεόντες, καὶ ἐπὶ ταῖς αὐταῖς στήλας περιπλεόντ, νήσων ἄρχουσι πασῶν, καὶ ἠπείρων ὅσαι καθήκουσιν ἐπὶ τ θάλασαν ὧν εἰσὶν ἐν δεξιᾷ προϊόντι Μαυρυσίων ὅσοι περὶ τ θά-

τίω Σικελίαν ἀψιμαχίαι πολλαῖ, ἔργου δὲ μείζονος ὀυδενός, Ταῦτη ὁ Καῖσαρ ἔπεμψε τὰς ἀρχὰς τῆ Πομπηίου προϊκόπλεν, καὶ τὰς πόλεις τὰς χορηγούσας προκαταλαμβάνειν. καὶ τῶ δὲ μάλιστα κάμνων ὁ Πομπήιος, ἔκρινε μάχη μείζονι κρίπηναι περὶ ἀπάντων· τὰ μὲν δὴ περὶ τῆ Καίσαρος ἐδεδίη, ταῖς τε ναυσὶν ἐπαγερόμβνος, ἤρετο πέμπων, εἰ δέχοιτο ναυμαχίᾳ κριθῆναι, ὁ δὲ, ὡρρώδη μὲν τὰς ἐν ἅλια πάντα, οὐ σὺν τύχη μέχρι δὲ ερχεχρημβνος αὖθις, αἰσχρὸν δὲ νομίσας ἀντειπεῖν, ἐδέχετο, ἢ ὠρίζετο αὖθις ἡ ἡμέρα, ἐς τὼ τειακόσιαι νῆες ἑκατέρα ἰδία προεσκδιάζοντο, βέλη τε πολλῆ τα φέρουσαι, καὶ πύργοις ἢ μηχαναῖς ὅσας ἐπενόοαν· ἐπενόει δὲ ὁ δὴ καλούμβνον ἅρπαγα ὁ Ἀγρίππας, ξύλον πεντάπηχυ σιδήρῳ περιεββλημβνον, κρίκοις ἔχον περὶ κεραίας ἑκατέρας, τῶν δὲ κρίκων εἷχεν, τῷ μὲν ὁ ἅρπαξ, σιδήρειον καμ-

La crainte de l'Eternel eſt le chef de ſcience: mais les fols meſpriſent ſapiéce &

Car ils ſeront graces enfilees enſemble à ton chef, & carquans à ton col. Mon fils, ſi les

them the 'French counterpart to the Italian *Cancellaresca*'.[69] Its first predecessor was based on a handwritten Gothic script used by merchants and notaries during the 16th century, which Robert Granjon initially called *lettre françoise*. A couple of years later, he designed an outwardly similar and even more successful variant, which was used in the children's manners manual, *La Civilité Puerile,* written by Erasmus. New editions of the book, always printed with the same style of type, made this title a synonym for the *Civilité* style.[70]

According to Plantin (its publisher), the typeface he purchased had 138 characters: upper-case and lower-case letters, ligatures, diacritics, punctuation marks, and abbreviations – as well as swash-formed initial and final letters. Additionally, Granjon made a matching musical notation system for a hymnal.

The *privilège du roi* permitting Robert Granjon to produce the type exclusively for ten years was already being violated after just two years when other printers started making derivatives in Paris. In 1571, the *Civilité* even arrived in Scotland, where it was introduced to printing under the name *Secretary.*

Into the 19th century, the *Civilité* typefaces were distributed by manufacturers (like Deberny et Peignot, Paris) in the same form as in the 16th century, even in the southern parts of Europe.[71] However, not all type designers remained true to the original design.*

In the 20th century, the advertising industry used some elements of the original *Civilité*. For instance, it was used to suggest the exotic atmosphere of the Middle East and the Far East. It saw rather little use in its original sense, e.g., for contexts related to the Middle Ages in northern Europe.[72]

Granjon set a 'milestone', as Max Caflisch called it, in 1565 with the *Litera Currens Ciceroniana,* alias *Pica Italic*.[73] The original typeface measured about 11 Didot points and differs from other italics created by Granjon in its having a shallower slope. The capitals are relatively small and thus allow for a calm, almost elegant appearance in text. This typeface first appeared in the 1565 book *Laertii Diogenis de vita et moribus philosophorum,* by Johannes Sambucus.* In 1964, Jan Tschichold used the *Pica Italic* as the model for his *Sabon Italic.*

*Morris Fuller Benton designed a typeface in 1922 that had little in common with Granjon's designs. However, this did not prevent the American Type Founders Company from selling the strictly Gothic-style typeface as *Civilité*.

*The *Pica Italic* on a type specimen sheet from Conrad Berner, Frankfurt, was called *Cursiff Parangon de Granjon.*

Argumentum Libri septi.

Septus Alexandrum luxu Babylonis et auro
Corruptum ostendit, castrensia munera certis
Distribuit numeris, armato milite fines
Yrios ingressus, Sizigambis liberat orbem,
Et Madatem precibus à moenibus eruta sumat
Inclita persepolis, monet occursus miserorum
Turbatum Regem, Darius discrimina martis
Rursus inire parat, hic seditio patricidas
Separat à Dario, Sed eos finnata simultas
Acceptos reddit, et pectora credula placat.
Nec fatum mutare valent decreta patronis.

C.   Liber

R	a a
B	b
C	c ç c ca ch ci co cr ct cu
D	d d d dd d dr dr d
E	c é c ci ty en em (ent) em (ent) er (er)
F	f ff [et (et) et (et) eu eu e (ez) t (&)
G	g g
H	h h
I	i iv (ie) ir (it) ir (it)
I	i
K	k
L	l l
M	m m m mm (me) mo (mo)
N	n n n no (no) n (nt)
O	o
P	p
Q	q
R	r t r w (re)
S	s s s ss ß
T	t t ta te tv (te) ti to tu tr tf (th)
V	u u s v v
W	w
X	x
Y	r y y yt (yt)
Z	z zr

Two similar italic typefaces followed, the *Philosophie Italique* and the *Italique Galliard droite*, as well as a third with much rounder forms, the *Petit Parangon Italique*. The latter measures 17 Didot points and was used in eight countries. Christoph Plantin in Antwerp used the type 1564 in the *Grammatica Hebraea*, for instance.

Of Granjon's great achievements, the *Italique sur la grosse Ascendonica* is worth mentioning here. In this typeface's appearance, the fast-working ductus of the nib appears to have been preserved almost completely. The inner and outer forms of the letters are so vivid and close to each other that they are barely perceptible and almost create an optical glimmer. The typeface was commissioned by Christoph Plantin in 1570 and it included a broad set of ligatures, swash capitals, etc. Its expansive forms were the inspiration for the *ITC Galliard* that Matthew Carter developed for photo-typesetting.* In his research, Carter also noted that Granjon was probably the first type designer to name his typefaces.[74]

* It should also be mentioned that Carter did not simply adopt the typeforms in detail, but in some cases gave himself greater freedom with the design.

Although Granjon created a considerable number of typefaces for Plantin, he also made a lot for himself, which he then sold to other interested parties. He was also famous for his arabesques, which he designed with dedication. Since Granjon was well-versed in the production of italics, it is obvious that he also produced Greek types, because their character was extremely similar to italic and demanded the greatest precision in their execution. Together with Pierre Haultin, Granjon was one of the best copyists of the *Grec du Roi*.[75] A specially designed *Parangon Grecque* contained more than two hundred characters and its design was on par with that of the *Grec du Roi*. His greatest legacy, however, remains the italics.

Anaxagoras Claz. *Post diutinam peregrinationem domum reuersus reperit patriam possessionesq́ suas desertas: Nisi, inquit, ista perissent, ego saluus non essem: Quòd calamitas illum adegisset ad philosophiam: Rebus autem integris, mansisset intra penates suos. Ita sæpenumerò prospera sunt homini, quæ videntur aduersa: & quod damnum putatur ingens, lucrum est maximum.*

{↗} The *Ascendonica Cursive*, cut by Robert Granjon for Christoph Plantin, whose steel punches and sets of matrices for four type sizes are kept in the *Plantin-Moretus Museum*

{→} The *Pica Italic* typeface on a type specimen from Conrad Berner, Frankfurt, featuring remarkably small caps (shown at 80 % size)

{↙} The *Petit Parangon Italique* shows eye-catching swash capitals. The Greek letters and the ornaments were also masterfully cut by Granjon (enlarged by 20 %)

Vtrum aliquid putamus mortem esse? Ita sane, respondit Simmias. Vtrum ergo, inquit ille, aliud quam animæ ac corporis putamus separationem esse? vt, nimirum, nihil aliud sit mori, quam vt corpus sit ab anima seiunctum, & seorsum sine hac existat: viciss̄ımque anima a corpore sit separata, eodemque modo, sola ac per se existat? Quæso, vtrum illud, an quid aliud ab illo est, quod mortem dicimus? Nihil, inquit ille, aliud profecto, sed hoc ipsum. Vide igitur, ô bone, vtrum idē nunc tibi, quod mihi, videatur. quippe hic facilius intelligemus illud, de quo inter nos nunc agimus. Vtrumne ergo munus esse existimas philosophi, addictum esse ijs voluptatibus, quæ è cibo aut è potu percipiuntur? Minime vero, o noster Socrates, respondit Simmias. Quid? ijsne, quæ è rebus Venereis petuntur? Nequaquam, inquit ille. Arbitraris ergo munus esse illius, vt in cultu corporis defixus hæreat? hoc est, vt exempli causa, vestes habeat eximias, aut calceos, aliaque id genus quæ ornando corpori excogitantur? Et vtrumne eum talia, aliaque id genus, admiraturum esse, an nullo habiturum loco, nisi quatenus necessitas id flagitat, existimas? Nullo ea loco si quid iudico, esse habiturum ; modo verus, inquit ille, sit philosophus. Nonne ergo prorsus sic videtur tibi, omne talis viri studium, non in corpore eiusque cura occupari, sed in id ei incumbendum, vt quantum potest, ab hoc faciat divortium, totumque se ad animum conuertat? Mihi quidem sane. Et an non ex ijs omnibus videtur tibi planum esse, eum qui revera sit philosophus, longe præ alijs a consortio corporis, seiuncturū esse animam? Videtur plane.

* In this adaptation, the integration of high stroke contrast became a characteristic feature, which is why the phrase 'letters with stroke contrast' is used for this section.

Letters with stroke contrast

Beginning in the last half of the 16th century, a slight renunciation of the Humanistic writing principles can be seen. Previously unconnected and upright letterforms were suddenly being written in a joined manner, with a slight slope or remarkable roundness. A corresponding typographic adaptation* followed somewhat later and was finally perfected to such an extent that the differences between handwritten and typographic forms became almost impossible to discern.[76] The first tendencies toward this appear in the work of the calligrapher Vespasiano Amphiareo, a Franciscan. Aside from a thirty-year teaching career, he produced a book in 1548 at Venice called *Un novo modo d'insegnar a scrivere et formar lettere di più sorti*. The sample writing style shown in this has shapes that are rounder and more open. Although Vespasiano derived his letters from mercantile handwriting, he still referred to those styles as 'monastic bastardas'.

The decisive impulses for a lasting writing-style rethink came from the Italian writing master Giovanni Francesco Cresci (died 1614). The historian A. S. Osley – who studied Cresci's calligraphy in the eighties – calls him a 'non-professional professional with a passionate interest in the technique of writing'. With this statement, he referred to Cresci's fundamental examination of the physical problems of writing by hand.[77]

In retrospect, it would not be an exaggeration to describe Cresci as a pioneer, because he dared to question the established writing practices of Arrighi and his contemporaries. Like Cresci's predecessors, he was also employed in the Vatican library and felt an urge to change the traditional style of the *Cancellaresca*. According to him, that upright handwriting style had become 'too lame and too heavy' or 'too bulky'.[78]

To achieve a fresher look, Cresci argued that letters should be written a little rounder and more narrowly with a pointed nib, and that they should join, or be connected. He recommended a much steeper degree of slope than was usual as well.[79] Cresci reinforced his concepts with the book *Il Perfetto Scittore* (The Perfect Writer). Numerous writing masters across Europe practised similar ideas for a broad and refined handwriting style. This marked the beginning of a new era for letters with stroke contrast.

Since then, a commercial standard in the writing ductus emerged, which initially sealed the fate of *Cancellaresca* cursives.[80] It was not until the 20th century that these Humanistic italics were revived, thanks to the pioneering work of calligraphers like Jan van de Velde, Edward Johnston and Tom Goudy.

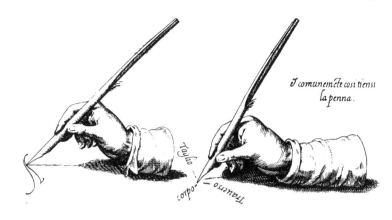

From a writing manual by Giuliantonio Hercolani, *Lo Scrittor Vtile*, 1574

The more fluent handwritten forms by Conretto da Monte Regale, 1576

From *Il perfetto scrittore*, Giovanni Francesco Cresci, 1570

Solo le virtù esaltano l'huomo al grado della gloria, et dell'honore, ne per altra via è possibile arriuare al tempio dell'Immortalità, et questo e il sentiero calcato da tutti i più famosi Heroi antichi, e moderni, C quatunque la strada sia fatigosa erta non però si sbigotisce l'animo generoso, conoscendo che dopo longa fatiga si gode il dolce prem

Il Conretto del Monte Regale di Piemonte Scriueua

Ad infiniti pericoli si espongono coloro che si lassano vincere dalle lusinghe de le donne, et da gli altri inhonesti apetiti, perche di questi piaceri non se ne caua altro, se non il tempo mal speso, la fama imbrattata, la robba consumata, il credito perduto, Iddio corrucciato, i vertuosi scandaleggiati. Inoltre i più disposti di vita diuentano ruffiani. & i più valorosi assassini di strada, i più viuaci d'ingegno pazzi, et i più accorti ladri. Però quelli che sono vestiti di più gratie naturali, et che per

The relocation of the printing centre in the direction of the Netherlands during the 17th century led to a flourishing of large printing dynasties, like those of the Plantin-Moretus, Elzevier, Blaeu and Wettstein families. Writing masters dominated the forms new typefaces would take and thus they determined the italic's future direction, too. Since then, italics have always been designed in a sophisticated and artistically pretentious manner, whether written or printed.[81] Significant developments in handwriting during the mid-17th century could also be observed in France, where three different handwriting trends came to the fore.

The first was called *Ronde* and it corresponded to the basic shapes of the *Civilité*, even though it was much lighter than the *Civilité's* heavy, Gothic forms.

The second one, called *Lettre Italienne,* was characterised by a writing method that was particularly round and connected. This kind of handwriting was first used by the papal scribe Lucas Materot from Avignon in his 1608 writing manual. A little later, the term *Copperplate* was applied to this style.

The third style had a similar ductus as the *Ronde* letterforms, but it was constructed out of even lighter and rounder shapes. A thinned-out variant of this style came to be known as *Lettre anglaise* or *English round-hand*.[82] In 1643, the punchcutter Pierre Moreau was the first to interpret these shapes typographically. Through 1648, these types were used in eleven books, where they were referred to by the term *Bâstardas italienne*.[83] These types were each designed progressively narrower and with increasingly greater slopes.

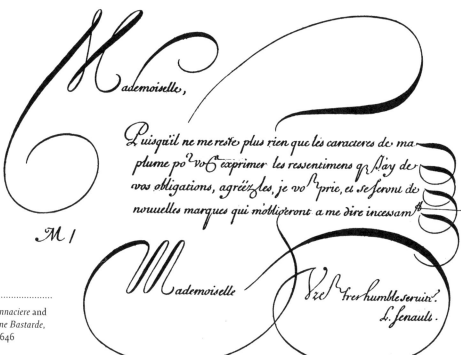

Mademoiselle,

Puisqu'il ne me reste plus rien que les caracteres de ma plume po[ur] vo[us] exprimer les ressentimens q[ue] j'ay de vos obligations, agréez les, je vo[us] prie, et se seront de nouuelles marques qui m'obligeront a me dire incessam[ent]

Mademoiselle   Vre tres humble seruiu[r].
                              L. Senault.

M 1

{↘} *Finnaciere* and *Italienne Bastarde*, Paris 1646

{↗} *Batârde coulée* by Louis Senault: *La Beauté de l'Escriture*, 1670

{↘} Page of a book by the writing master Edward Cocker, 1657

Oh! if such beaming Lustre's in Arts Face.
What Beauties, what Perfections, are in Grace?
If in Grace more, what may in Glorie bee?
O, infinitelie more! but what in Thee
Lord, who dost all Transcendencies transcend!
Who beginne t'admire Thee nere shall End!
Hic Modus est non habuisse Modum.

BONTÉ
—
DESIR.

C'eſt le ſujet de cette Médaille. On y voit Pallas, tenant un Javelot preſt à lancer; le fleuve de l'Eſcauld effrayé s'appuye ſur ſon Urne. La Légende, HISPANIS TRANS SCALDIM PULSIS ET FUGATIS, ſignifie, *les Eſpagnols défaits & pouſſez au-delà de l'Eſcauld.* L'Exergue, CONDATUM ET MALBODIUM CAPTA. M. DC. XLIX. *priſe de Condé & de Maubeuge. 1649.*

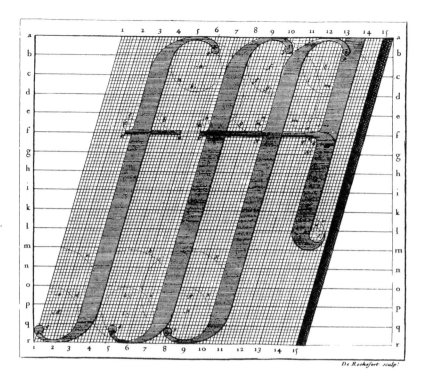

{←} Grandjean's
Roman du Roi,
produced between
1692 and 1714

{→} The italic
characters of the
Romain du Roi are
based on a diagonal
grid system.

During the Baroque era, italics were increasingly dominated by their subordi-
nation to roman type and they lost their independence as text faces. This
tendency first became noticeable on the design of title pages or at the beginning
of chapters. Gradually, italics came to be used for emphasis within roman
texts.[84] The first real duo of both type styles *(roman* and *italic)* was the *Romain
du Roi* typeface, which was designed at the behest of King Louis XIV by the
Academy of Sciences and which is largely based on geometric principles.
That concept was even applied to the italics, which were designed on an oblique
grid. However, the implementation of this design did not adhere to those
models very rigidly. The punchcutter at the Imprimerie Royale, Phillippe
Granjean de Fouchy, received the commission to produce the punches according
to a series of outline drawings but had no method of reducing those down to
type size. Once the typeface was finished, a royal decree was issued to restrict
its use, but this was quickly violated by multiple printers. The *Romain du Roi*
became the established standard for punchcutters and printers in France.
In 1702, the first book to be printed with the new types was published. This
was the *Médailles sur les principaux événements du régne de Louis le Grand.* [85]

illis plurima dixerimus, multo plura adhuc superesse dicenda ne ipse quidem livor inficiari possit. Qua de re manum de tabula tollimus *Vir Nobilissime & Gravissime*, &, ut novam hanc *Salmasii Exercitationum in Solinum Plinianarum* editionem vultu sereno & placido accipias, rogamus. Afferimus Tibi quod possumus, dum non licet quod volumus, opus non quidem nostro elaboratum ingenio, nostris tamen descriptum typis. Quod ubi Tibi non displicere intellexerimus, lætabimur, & ut divini numinis plenus Reipublicæ Ultrajectinæ rem bene geras, & serus in cœlum redeas, Deum ter Optimum Maximum supplices venerabimur.

Vir Nobilissime & Gravissime,
   clientes Tibi devotissimi,

264 VIE DE M. DE FÉNÉLON.

humilier ou nous confondre, ne paroît occupé que de nos intérêts et de notre bonheur.

Fénélon vouloit que toutes les affaires de son diocese lui fussent rapportées, et il les examinoit par lui-même; mais la moindre chose importante dans la discipline ne se décidoit que de concert avec ses vicaires généraux et les autres chanoines de son conseil, qui s'assembloit deux fois la semaine. Jamais il ne s'y est prévalu de son rang ou de ses talents, pour décider par autorité, sans persuasion : il reconnoissoit les prêtres pour ses freres, recevoit leurs avis, et profitoit de leur expérience. *Le pasteur,* disoit-il, *a besoin d'être encore plus docile que le troupeau; il faut qu'il apprenne sans cesse pour enseigner, qu'il obéisse souvent pour bien commander. Le sage agrandit sa sagesse par toute celle qu'il recueille en autrui.*

Il ne se contentoit pas de faire les fonctions éminentes de l'épiscopat, il exerçoit même celles d'un prêtre ordinaire, en confessant, en dirigeant quantité de laïques qui étoient soumis à sa conduite. On a imprimé, depuis sa mort, un recueil de lettres auxquelles nous en ajouterons beaucoup d'autres, qu'il a écrites aux personnes qui le consultoient. On verra et la confiance qu'elles avoient dans ses lumieres et dans sa bonté, et combien dans sa pratique il étoit éloigné de tourner la spiritualité dans une spéculation seche,

These two page excerpts from different books call back to the point just after italics had finally been established as a secondary style.

{←} Roman type by Christopher van Dijck paired in 1689 with Granjon's *Parangon italic* (20% reduced)

{→} Acclaimed by Morison, this is the formal yet elegant italic by François Ambrois Didot, 1785

....

At the end of the 17th century, the writing of highly stylistic and complex forms was being cultivated. This was not only due to the aesthetic preferences of that age's calligraphers but also for professional reasons. According to Stanley Morison, some calligraphers were interested in making their styles particularly difficult to learn, to protect their professional position and allow them to publish writing manuals of their own. One person who exemplified this practice was Edward Cocker, who was as successful as an engraver as he was as a professional scribe.[86] The English writer and engraver Gabriel Brooks also strove for perfection.[87] His works reflect a methodically-precise approach, in which every detail and every connecting piece was worked out with delicate precision, letter by letter.

The increasing thirst for knowledge and investigation of the time was also reflected in finer writing styles. Meanwhile, pointed nibs and etching needles had become indispensable instruments in type design. Writing itself began to gain an unachievable level of sophistication. A next logical step could only be the integration of these virtuoso styles into typography. In comparison with some of the highly technical text varieties that had been in place until then, these offered a strong contrast.

From then on, the task was not only to design a text with a basic, typographically-structured relationship but also to give it the character of a handwritten text. The hand of the scribe was thus imitated by printed letters. In the end, entire epistles looking as if they had been handwritten would come press just as easily from the printing.

Between 1750 and 1800, while English colonies were spreading across the world, the *English copperplate* maintained its dominant position. Later, French, Spanish and even Italian writing schools began including that style in their repertoire. It was also used in the young United States of America.

Pierre Simon Fournier (1712 – 1768), the creator of the *Fournier* point system (and the round musical notation printing type), shows a typical French *Ronde* inside his *Modèles des caractères de l'imprimerie,* in his 1740 work *Caractère de finance, dit Bâtarde Coulée,* and in his *Manuel Typographique* of 1763.[88] Giambattista Bodoni concerned himself with the translation of handwriting into print extensively, too. This gave rise to a typeface genre that is referred to today as *script* and which takes many variations and forms (page 21 f.)

At the beginning of the 19th century, several other kinds of *script* typefaces arose, which all showed an astonishing similarity to handwriting. Three examples are shown on the opposite page.

Lettres Ornées,

Pour tenire lieu & petites Capitales dans le Caractere de FINANCE, dix Batarde Coulée. Gravé par Fournier le jeune.

61   *Bâtarde Coulée* by Pierre Simon Fournier, 1749

There are many shining Qualities in the Minds of Men, but there is none so useful as Discretion; it is this indeed which gives a Value to all the rest, which sets them at Work in their proper Times and Places, & turns them to the Advantage of the Person who is possessed of them.

62   This copperplate engraving is based on the form of an *English round-hand* that was frequently used during the 18th century; by Gabriel Brooks, 1737.

Homme, sois bien humain, aime constamment les Arts, tu vivras heureux Il vaut mieux être dupe plutôt que d'être ingrat.

63   A typographisised *Grosse Bâtarde Creuse* from Allain Guillaume, 1808

Developments through the present day

The last two hundred years have seen turbulent development, interspersed by undefined shifts in direction within this style. The more influence that technical changes had on people, the more that the typographic expectations and requirements on italic typefaces increased. Beyond this, innovations in printing and manufacturing technology also drove typeface production forward. The personal computer comes at the end of this chain of events, which made it easier for anyone interested to freely design typefaces with comparatively little effort and at a low cost. As a result, we are now confronted with a range of typefaces in both high and inferior levels of quality. To reconstruct recent history in a comprehensible way, I will limit myself to the most important details.

During the 1820s, the structure of italic typefaces' outward appearance changed dramatically. Traditional forms that had origination in handwriting were suddenly abandoned and replaced by mechanically-slanted forms. The German engraver Gustav Friedrich Ermeler created one of the first *sloped-roman* italic-style typefaces. An 1820 specimen of that appears on the next page.

Even if the reasons for the emergence of these *sloped romans* is still unclear, it is possible to determine what effects they had. After the first sans serif typefaces had been created, the principle of slanting a typeface's letters was applied in that new genre as well. The first sans serif italics that have been found were all obliqued designs, a situation that influenced the further development of sans serif italic type even through the present day. An American type specimen from 1840 shows that – from a type designer's point of view – 'italicising' could even offer new creative possibilities.

POËTES.

Malherbe, P. Corneille, Th. Corneille,
Racine, Boileau-Despreaux, La Fontaine,
Molière, Crébillon, Malfilatre, Voltaire,
Pyron, Le-Brun, le C.al de *Bernis,* 1Ab. *Delille.*

{←} A lithographi-cally-printed business card from the middle of the 19th century

{→} Obliqued lower-case letters in an italic typeface by Gustav Friedrich Ermeler, 1820

USTER RED hunder

Early sans serif italics with different slopes, 1840

These sans serifs were supplemented by another italic style sloped in the opposite direction, which was presumably used for advertising purposes. The Swiss typographer and author Jost Hochuli cites 'drawn lithographic lettering' as a source of inspiration for obliqued lower-case letters.[89]

In this context, upheavals of the industrial age must also be taken into account: the more that industry, the economy and trade flourished during the 19th century, the greater the number of type foundries in operation grew. Professional groups like lithographers and engravers also stimulated the type sector.[90] The abundance of type specimen from this time that survived into the present suggests that a massive influx of people entered the type-founding industry. To remain viable, individual manufacturers had to rely on new type designs. They increased the number of products they offered and began including unconventional design ideas in their specimens, like typefaces with obliqued lower-case letters.

In the 1890s, the emergence of new italic typefaces – at least for serif products – came to a halt again. Preference was given to advertising typefaces based on artists' drawings. The type foundries tied their hopes to this and invested a lot of energy, time and financial resources producing that new kind of product. But the desired success did not come – except in a few cases. Hermann Zapf commented that 'although the world of advertising always demanded new, eye-catching styles, the influence of those typefaces was minimal. After all, such desires were often subject to rapidly-changing fashion trends. Too much variation of the basic shapes, or too much emphasis on the peculiarities of the pen stroke, soon led to the conclusion that these typefaces were too difficult for printers to combine, ruling out their broad applicability.'[91]

gs gs
gs gs
gs gs

67 According to
the London-based
typographer and
publisher Robin
Kinross, 'italic
means more than
just inclined to the
right'. Regarding
the image shown
above, he asks 'if
a sloped roman
is more logical than
an italic, is it as
satisfying visually
and semantically?'[93]

This was followed by a return to the italic's natural source – handwriting – and important calligraphers like Edward Johnston (1872 – 1944) provided ground-breaking contributions. His textbooks, including *Writing and Illuminating and Lettering* (1906), emphasised the relationships between handwriting and printing typefaces, contributing to a calligraphic revival. In particular, that book was successful. It was reprinted many times and republished in multiple editions. Anna Simons, a student of his, also translated the book into German in 1910.

During the 1920s, another adjustment was applied, this time under the direction of the renowned theorist Stanley Morison (1889 – 1967), who would go on to become the father of the *Times New Roman* typeface.[92] Some typographers found his suggestion for obliqued *sloped-roman* italics controversial, and a great deal of discussion and debate resulted. Morison published the well-known article 'Towards an Ideal Italic' the fifth issue of his journal *The Fleuron* in 1926. Although the theses he put forward there represented a return to past practices, the article was the first independent approach to the question of the conditions of the italic's proper appearance on a theoretical level.

Over thirty pages, Morison first reconstructed the transformation of calligraphic styles into italic type through to the multitude of connecting typefaces produced during the 18th century. An important part of the article addresses the evaluation of capital letters. Morison even tried to evaluate distinguished examples from the history of italic type. He wrote about those from a primarily typographic point of view, judging them by their relation-ships to their companion text (or roman) typefaces. According to him, italics simply could not be judged in a manner isolated from that context.

For example, he referred to Grandjean's *Romain du Roi* as the first specific italic. He recommended an italic cut by François Ambroise Didot (1730 – 1804) as the best example of how a formal italic could be constructed, although he regretted the calligraphic residue remaining in the typeface.[94]

In the article's second part, Morison put the only alternative he supported forward: it was *sloped-roman* types that should be used when italics were needed. To back this up, he advanced a series of plausible arguments. For instance, existing italic forms seem to be 'essentially incompatible' with the basic typeface (romans); Morison declared that the classic typeface family was unharmonious. He used strict language to explain this, writing that 'since the roman is the text type it follows that to retain complete the cursive nature of the italic and at the same time demand harmony in the page is to ask the impossible'. He concluded from this that an italic design could only be acceptable if it kept to the design of a roman as closely as possible.

It is therefore our business carefully to *cultivate* in our minds, to rear to the most

m n p u v w

m n p u v w

m n p u v w

a b b c c f f

h k l l m p y

A H M R W

68   A special *sloped-roman* italic for *Caslon,* shown in Morison's 1926 article.

This ken we truly, that as wonder to intellect,
so for the soul desire of beaty is mover and spring;
whence, in whatever his spirit is most moved, a man
wil most be engaged with beauty; and thus in his
'first love' physical beauty and spiritual are both presen
mingled inseprarably in his lure: then is he seen
in the ecstasy of earthly passion and of heavenly vision
to fall to idolatry of some specious appearance
as if 'twer very incarnation of his heart's desire,
whether eternal and spiritual, as with Dance it was,
or mere sensuous perfection, or as most commanly
a fusion of both — when if distractedly he hav thought
to mare mortally with an eternal essence
all the delinquencies of his high passion ensue.

ABCDEFGHIJK
LMNOPQRSTU
VWXYZ
abcdefghijklmnopq
qrstuvwxyz &abcdef
ghijklmnopqrstuvwxyz
1234567890

Additionally, Morison took the decline of writing out texts by hand into account, which was then already in progress. He believed that this was a sign of an unfolding rearrangement in typography and demanded that about eighty per cent of the historical 'burden' be removed from traditional italics.

As for Morison's radical considerations, the renowned Swiss typographer Max Caflisch considered that a 1903 alphabet for stonemasons from Eric Gill (1882 – 1940) had provided the first impetus guiding his approach in this direction. Already in 1925, Morison persuaded Gill to begin working on the typeface that would eventually be published by the Monotype Corporation Inc. as *Perpetua*.[95] Gill completed his first drafts for its roman that same year, as well as for its italic, which was initially known by the name *Felicity*. After Gill turned his final drawings over to Morison, the Parisian punchcutter Charles Malin was commissioned to cut trial punches for the typeface in steel. In Morison's opinion, the first results were not convincing enough; the typeface still contained too many calligraphic elements and needed to be further 'disciplined'. Although Morison proposed a pure *sloped roman* – which Gill agreed to – the resulting italic design was more like 'a series of compromises'.[96] Despite that, in a follow-up article to *The Fleuron* in 1930, Morison attempted to further consolidate his theory by putting *Perpetua* forward as an example. Here, he succeeded because the American typographic publicist Beatrice Warde (1900 – 1969) – alias Paul Beaujon – wrote that '*Perpetua italic* ... interestingly carries out the prediction first made in the fifth number of *The Fleuron* that, if the italic is to develop into a contemporary form, consistency demands that it should no longer retain the calligraphic peculiarities derived from a school of writing quite different from that of the roman; that it must, in fact, become frankly the italic *of* the given roman, with only slope, and the modifications necessary to slope, to distinguish it from the upright version'.[97]

However, critics see *Perpetua* as the failure of that ideal. Walter Tracy explained in *Letters of Credit* that *Perpetua* does not embody an uncompromising *sloped-roman* ideal, because it can – at best – be described as a hybrid. Tracy justified his conclusion by arguing that the designs of its letterforms were too inconsistent. Significant features of *Perpetua's* italic are the letters *m* and *n*, which look just like roman letterforms, even though they are sloped. However, the designs for the letters *a, e,* and *g* look calligraphic instead.[98]

At about the same time, Gill completed the design for a second typeface family the Monotype Corporation would produce. Although this resembled *Perpetua* in many of its details, it was not a serif typeface, but a sans serif. However, a direct connection between the two typeface's developments is still conceivable. The latter design was completed in 1930 and marketed under the name *Gill Sans Titling* (eventually shortened to *Gill Sans)*.

{←} *Perpetua* with its companion italic, originally named *Felicity*, 1926

162   *Margaret B. Evans*

Laurance Siegfried and I printed the first two issues,
removal announcement and the Occasional Bulleti.
That was the origin of the Püterschein myth. Lauranc
was Jacob and I was Hermann. In looking up the fami
tree Jacob found some female relatives, Henrietta, He
wig and Elsa.

Note the discovery of those female relatives. Georg
Meredith, in his *Essay on Comedy*, remarked: "The
has been fun in Bagdad. But there never will be civi
zation where comedy is not possible; and that comes o
some degree of social equality of the sexes." Here, wit
the participation of female Püterschein relatives, bega
several decades of civilized fun in Hingham, Mass.

1916-1917

VAGUE. Written and illustrated in collaboration wit
John Phillips, Jr., Edward O'Brien and Harrison I
Cowan.

You might call that an escape effort on the part o
three of us. We just had fun with Amy Lowell and poly
phonic prose.

1917

SONNETS AND OTHER LYRICS, by Robert Silliman Hillye
Harvard University Press.

The first trade book I ever designed in type....

1921

THE WITCH WOLF, by Joel Chandler Harris. Bacon an
Brown.

We did it for an imaginary firm that Chester Lan
was running. That rabbit is a darned good drawing

{→} Significant differences in the structure of the lower-case *a*, from various *Gill Sans* styles, 1930

{↘} For comparison, see the more schematic construction of the *Univers* family, designed by Adrian Frutiger, 1957

{←} *Electra* with two differend italics, 1935

What was criticized as 'too much' in *Perpetua* was finally celebrated as a novelty in *Gill Sans*. That typeface was the first sans serif to have been designed with Humanistic characteristics. As with *Perpetua*, the italic styles in *Gill Sans* had forms for the letters *a*, *g* and *p* designed with shapes common in older italic typefaces. Eric Gill was ahead of his time. For the next thirty years, *Gill Sans* was the only sans serif with Humanist forms, at least among the many newly-developed sans serif families. Other sans serif italics – like those in *Univers*, which had been systematically designed by Adrian Frutiger in 1957, or in Hans Eduard Meier's 1972 *Syntax* – had sloped letters as their italics' main characteristic. But the enthusiasm for obliqued lower-case letters soon subsided, and even Morison himself would finally give up on the idea. What remained was the recommendation of a technically-prominent person, whose statements were able to influence even well-known typographers like Jan van Krimpen or William Addison Dwiggins* (WAD).

* In his 1922 newspaper article 'New Kinds of Printing Calls for New Design', WAD used the term *graphic design* for the first time to describe *printing for purpose* precisely. **99**

The work of WAD testifies to his great enthusiasm for experimentation. Perhaps unsurprisingly, WAD also decided to put the *sloped roman* into practice. Dwiggins' *Electra* typeface used *sloped-roman* features in its italics – although some concessions were necessary for an italic's character to be preserved. He was unable to avoid keeping several traditional forms, including a fluid *f*, a round *a* and a curved *e*.

In this context, I would like to reference a book published in 1960, entitled *Postscripts on Dwiggins*. This charmingly illustrated Dwiggins' capabilities and revealed an interesting way of applying emphasis. Titles were set with a traditional cursive-style italic and a *sloped roman* was used for quotations.[100] Additionally, the book included an almost-upright yet free-flowing cursive typeface. It is of interest in-so-far-as it seems to represent the opposite of Morison's ideas. It is not certain whether that was why the typeface – called *Charter* – was never published. Dwiggins did not design it until 1937 (so, after Morison's theses had fallen out of fashion). It embodies an upright, almost left-leaning italic.

Sibylle Hagmann, a Swiss typographer living in the USA, made an important contribution to its revival. In 2007, she published a theoretical piece on Dwiggins in the Swiss magazine *Typografische Monatsblätter*.[101] A year earlier, She had designed a serif typeface named *Odile* that included upright italics inspired by *Charter*.

Indirectly, therefore, the *sloped-roman* lower-case could be preserved. Apart from the rise of sans serif typefaces, some technical inventions in the field of printing even temporarily boosted their popularity, too. Simple manipulation of a roman font with typesetting tools could result in mechanically generated italics. Such a technique was already integrated into photo-typesetting machinery by in the 1950s. By adjusting special lenses, it was possible to alter the projection of 'normal' letters so that they would become 'narrow' or 'wide' instead. Rotating the lenses could add distortion and thus artificially slope the letters by up to 12 degrees in either direction. The printing industry greeted devices that could do this as a welcome technical change. During the introduction of CRT typesetting systems in newspaper publishing, this technique was initially applied because of a lack of real italic fonts being available for the first generations of those machines. Automatically-generated results seemed acceptable enough for the printers to use in place of real italics in newspapers.[102] By the time that the machines improved to allow them to have more fonts installed at the same time, the use of 'fake italics' had already become a standard, at least in newspaper printing. This example illustrates how much the typographic eye's tolerance for formality determines a typeface's design.

73 {→} *Charter,* upright italic by W. A. Dwiggins, 1937

74 {↘} Illustration showing how control of the lens in CRT photo-type-setting could manipulate a letter-form, including its slope (1950)

This special-purpose face, later named Charter, was conceived early in 1937, when a few trial characters were cut for evaluation. In the Summer of 1942 the project was revived and drawings made for the lower-case alphabet. At that time, WAD thought of a decorative cap letter that might be used in place of, or as a supplement to, the customary script capital. Trial drawings were made of an ornamented 𝔉 and 𝔙, and also a script 𝔐 and ℬ for appraisal. Though the effect was "most promising," no additional drawings of either form were received.

An early specimen attempt, equally promising, combined the normal roman capitals of Electra (as used here) with the Charter script lowercase. The text for this piece was that of the first Thanksgiving Proclamation, at Charlestown, Mass., dated June 20, 1676. Script numerals to match the height of the round lowercase letters, with a width approximating that of the lowercase "h," were then planned.

The first experimental use of the face in book form, purposely uncredited, was made in the limited edition of "The Song Story of Aucassin and Nicolete," designed and printed by S. A. Jacobs in 1946, at the Golden Eagle Press, Mount Vernon, New York. For this text, Electra small caps were used in place of

Since the middle of the 1950s, contemporary typography has mainly been characterized by derivatives of italic variants made earlier in the past. The experiences of past centuries show just how strong the influence of Humanist italics was. They inspired yet another generation of typefaces. Jan van Krimpen's Spectrum (1952), Jan Tschichold's *Sabon* (1967) and Bram de Does' *Trinité* (1980) are some of the more prominent examples of this.

In the 1980s, a change in thinking also came about for sans serif typefaces. One example of this is *Flora*, designed by Gerard Unger in 1984. *Flora* is an extremely minimal typeface. Its forms are based on writing, but its strokes are monolinear. The analytical approach to the typeface's design is particularly interesting. Unger examined the relationships between letters' widths, stroke thicknesses and slopes in detail. Finally, he designed a broad family whose italics were equipped with different degrees of inclination. *Today Sans* by Volker Küster (1988) should also be mentioned for its modern approach to sans serif design, including the Humanist appearance of its italics.

The current generation of type designers has more possibilities, but also far more typefaces. These days, we live in a time when type designers can use PCs or Macs to freely bring their ideas about. Using these machines, they shape the designs of letters, determine the amount of space coming before and after them, and define the kerning – i.e., spacing adjustments between individual letter pairs. In brief, they make fonts that can be used by typographers for almost any purpose. To gain the consumer's goodwill, however, we have to follow conventions. For users of type, historical aspects are still present and important. So it is not surprising that popular typefaces adhere to traditional 'values'. The italics in *FF Quadraat* (1992, Fred Smeijers), for instance, are based on punchcutters' shapes. On the other hand, *FF Scala* (1991, Martin Majoor) follows examples set by writing masters. Traditional forms are still used in serif typefaces today, and this will most likely be true for decades to come.

The development process for italics has never stopped. It regularly returns to the experiments of the old master calligraphers and punchcutters, whose ways of using them depended on the writing tools they had available. To explain this more deeply, I will now take you to an examination of how italic forms are constructed.

Today Sans
Volker Küster, 1988

**This ken we truly, that as wonder to intellect,
so for the soul desire of beaty is mover and spring;**

Flora
Gerard Unger, 1984

whence, in whatever his spirit is most moved, a man
wil most be engaged with beauty; and thus in his

75 Sans serif italics with traditionally-designed lower-case letters

Spectrum
Jan van Krimpen, 1952

*'first love' physical beauty and spiritual are both present
mingled inseprarably in his lure: then is he seen*

Trinité
Bram de Does, 1980

*in the ecstasy of earthly passion and of heavenly vision
to fall to idolatry of some specious appearance*

76 Classic Humanist-style italics

FF Scala
Martin Majoor, 1992

*as if 'twer very incarnation of his heart's desire,
whether eternal and spiritual, as with Dance it was,*

FF Quadraat
Fred Smeijers, 1991

*or mere sensuous perfection, or as most commanly
a fusion of both — when if distractedly he hav thought*

77 Modern traditional-style italics, influenced by older handcraft techniques

OTF Lirico
Hendrik Weber, 2008

*to mare mortally with an eternal essence
all the delinquencies of his high passion ensure.*

78 Modern neo-Humanist italics

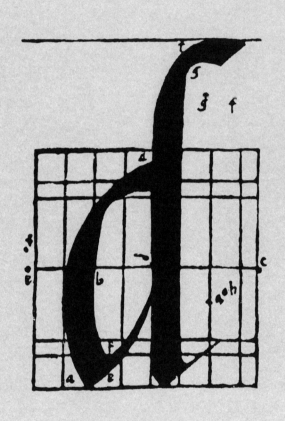

....

Constructing the form

This last, more practically-oriented part of the book explores the anatomical structures that italics take. The historical basics presented earlier explained how writing tools were used so the question now is what significance they had for the designs of various typefaces.

In the '*basic elements of the letterforms*' section, the interaction of specific features like '*ductus, speed and character*' will be scrutinised. The aim here is to decode the italic style's relationships, step by step. In the '*lower-case letters*' and '*capitals*' sections, that the information is transferred to the letters' construction. Finally, a fundamental assessment of the italic's character is given.

Writing instruments and their traces

'A typeface will always be subject to optical rules because pure construction does not exist. Even a sans serif must submit to the laws of optics, for it is still the human eye that ingests the letters, not an electronic device.' [103] This statement from Hermann Zapf refers to the independent optical existence of the written word and its appearance. That is what the following section is concerned with.

Every basic form of applied lettering is characterised by the nature of the tool used to write it. For the Chinese script, it was the brush; for the Arabic, Hebrew and Latin scripts, it was the broad nib. Even the carved letters of the Roman *Capitalis* originally followed figures drawn with a flat brush. As a result of typographical adaptations, letter designs were standardised. They were either engraved into wood, copper or steel. They were reproduced in letterpress printing with cast-metal letters. Even though the printers oriented themselves toward handwritten models, the traces of the above-mentioned procedures remained recognizable in the characters of the typefaces they used.

....

{ P. 84 } Shop
lettering in
Brushfield Street,
London

{ ↖ } Drawing by
Ferdinando Ruano
showing a con-
structed letterform,
1554

....

In contrast to the strokes drawn with a pen, the wielding of a graver or an etching needle was a partial process granting certain freedom beyond what the pen could allow. Typefaces that were created in this way were formally mature and more precisely defined than written letters. Some alphabets engraved in copper approached such a degree of perfection that they even surpassed written originals.[104]

With the help of computer technology, this trend is basically continuing. However, working on a monitor is by no means comparable to manual practice. The screen merely reproduces a digital image that redefines working possibilities far away from real conditions. Despite laptops, computers remain rather inflexible tools that are dependent on the input of the designer and which are connected to any drawing capabilities the user may have. The mouse – an interface that cannot replace either the pen nor a pencil – just functions as a technical aid instead.

Nevertheless, I consider Macs, PCs, etc. to be forward-looking tools that guarantee time-efficient and flawless implementation of type. However, the advantages that can be identified only become apparent in the way the tasks are distributed, in which the creative, spontaneous or process-oriented idea-finding is still reserved for the pencil and/or pen.

Although both tool types have certain similarities, learning to write – from a qualitative point of view – inevitably leads to the use of the pen. The tip of a pencil is too undefined at a higher writing level; its trace leads to an elongated dot or line. The use of a pen nib, however, can shape the long surface of a stroke. This stroke can also be controlled by shifting or rotating the writing instrument. In total, there are three types of pens whose traces have shaped typography: broad, pointed and round.

The Humanistic typefaces have their roots in the stroke patterns made by a *broad pen* (Fig. 80), whose ductus is similar to that of a flat brush. The tip of the broad pen has a fixed width, which is drawn across the surface at a pre-determined angle ranging between 30 and 45 degrees. Even a slight twist of the pen's tip will alter the ratio between the widths of the vertical and horizontal strokes. When drawing a curve, the stroke thickness narrows or widens depending on the direction. The contrast axis inside a circle – which is 90 degrees from the tip of the nib – is slanted.

The use of the pointed pen (Fig. 81) led to more contrasting and narrow letters, beginning in the middle of the 17th century. A single stroke, no matter in which direction it is drawn, is usually equally as thin. The application of pressure to the tip of the nib defines what intensity any contrast will have. Pressure spreads the two halves of the nib outward and the flowing ink is

81 Writing with the round pen

82 Principle of the broad pen and the flat brush

83 Pointed-pen writing results in greater contrast

distributed over a wider stroke area. Writing with a pointed pen requires certain knowledge about the contrast relationships it can generate for strokes and the proprieties of the writing practices that have typically employed this instrument. Usually, the vertical strokes are more strongly emphasised than horizontal or diagonal ones. For this reason, the contrast axis in a circle is vertical.

A *Redis* nib (Fig. 82) has a circular plate for its tip so that the stroke thickness is basically the same regardless of the direction of movement. For this reason, it plays a special role, allowing it to be used in more technically-oriented areas. A circle drawn with the *Redis* nib creates a contrast-less, almost geometric shape.

The following explanation primarily focuses on the principle of broad-nib writing, which the majority of all book typefaces follow. Their contrast model is one of the most striking characteristic features of writing it and therefore holds a special place in typography.

Basic elements of the letterforms
Writing by hand gives a stroke characteristic features, i.e., a first and fundamental structure. According to Fred Smeijers' considerations, there are three
different ways it can be placed:

1 The scratch-stroke is the result of a short, rapidly-made movement and the path it will
take is not entirely predictable.

2 The stroke carried out with concentration is deliberately controlled by the slow-moving
hand.

3 The 'experienced' stroke combines both of the above-mentioned varieties. It is made
neither too slowly nor too quickly. It has its particular look here because its movement-
direction has changed twice.

Of course, it is possible to write with all three of these styles. However, the
differences between expression and writing efficiency are significant. Writing
is a rhythmic sequence of individual, varying strokes.[105] This is a rather
complex process that starts in the head, long before finally reaching the page.
Individual factors such as vitality, posture or arm movement can influence
letterforms just as much as the choice of materials or tools. When writing, one
tries to make the letter structure amenable with the help of vital and mechanical
capabilities. Together with the brain, the eye takes control of the arm, hand,
finger, pen and even the shape. This sequence is rarely proportional in its
application – the exception is the 'experienced' stroke. At writing speeds where
the strokes follow one another too quickly (1) the activity becomes difficult
for the brain to follow, as it can hardly keep up with sensory capabilities of
a hurrying hand. A rather slow procedure (2) requires a lot of time, which
means: absolute concentration and consistent motor-skill control over the
arm. The 'experienced' stroke (3) fully controls the balanced relative strength
between tempo and rhythm during the writing process.

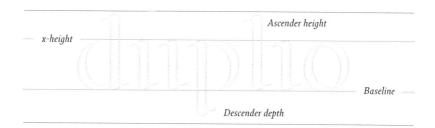

Functionality of
an 'experienced'
stroke

A preliminary warm-up period is the most important condition for routine
writing. Once the writing rhythm has been internally absorbed, the subsequent
application has noticeably more balanced forms. Even a faster tempo becomes
controllable and factors such as writing rhythm, letter height and overall
texture are balanced out almost casually.

This most efficient variant of a stroke is divided into three parts. The upper
part, the in-stroke (a) begins with a slow turn, followed by a faster middle
section, the stem (b). The last part at the bottom, the out-stroke (c), is the most
significant; it slows down again with a slight sideways movement by the
writing instrument. This pattern of combined movement sequence has dominated writing habits for the last thousand years and thus also influenced the
very core of the development of cursive writing styles. It is the driving force
behind the italic. [106]

Even the forms of the serifs in roman typefaces can be traced back to this
mechanism. The classic double serif merely corresponded to a variation of the
'experienced' stroke, which was created by adding a stroke. The mere sequence
of the 'experienced' stroke, on the other hand, corresponds to the *natural*
(relaxed) movement of the writing instrument and creates so-called *natural*
serifs.

Within the overall texture of a text, the alternating strokes are supported
by further basic elements such as rounds or ascenders and descenders, which
are subject to the same formal principles. In the example shown above, these
elements fit perfectly into the overall structure and provide the necessary
distinctiveness between characters for readers.

....

Construction

In most letters, the separate partial strokes merge into one construction. Generally speaking, there are three possibilities for this:

A  B

....

A An *interrupted construction* is dominated by one-side execution, in which the tool is put down and writing continues again later, from a suitable position.

B In a *returning* (or *running*) construction, the pen is not put down. Instead, the direction of movement changes and the movement of the stroke simply continues in that new direction.

C The third construction represents neither an *interrupted* nor a *connected* stroke. Instead, it is a sophisticated interpretation of a *running construction*, in which the strike movement is interrupted.

C

Every culture knows *interrupted* (A) and *returning* constructions (B). In the
Japanese script, for instance, *kaisho* is interrupted and *gyousho* is returning.[107]
In western scripts the roman is the most common example for an interrupted
variant, while a returning construction is at the core of cursive styles. The
typographical landscape, however, is primarily dominated by italics that are
moulded and therefore conventional-looking. Their structure is also interrupted (C).[108] The reasons for this are partly to be found in the objectification
of the printing process and improvements made for text-image legibility.
The *running* style of handwriting is based on a free or casual executability.
Due to this more direct approach, *connected* constructions consist of much
fewer single strokes than *interrupted* ones. A *connected* n can be written
with a single pen stroke. For an *interrupted* n, on the other hand, two strokes
are needed, and a *g* even needs five partial strokes.

These simplifications were developed primarily to enable quicker text
transcription. It was only a matter of time before corresponding stylistic
adaptations were made within the script. Moreover, the process was anything
but consistent. Constructions were often mixed.

However, the *running* or natural construction did not always have to
satisfy the exclusive purpose of consistent practicability, which is why both
kinds of construction continue to exist side-by-side to this day.

Apart from these constructions, so-called *bastards* developed as exceptions, since they did not fit into either of the other two groups. Although they
look very clearly interrupted, they were written on a running basis. Their style

....

is based on a frequent change of direction, which gives text written with them a halting instead of a connected look.

These hybrid forms developed during the Gothic period and established themselves as mercantile writing styles alongside the *Textura*. However, if one compares the hybrid forms with a Textura, one can see that they contain fluid elements. Thus, early running constructions were not always used for efficiency reasons, but also stylistic ones. *Civilités* are among the related examples from the Gothic italics.

A text that is written out entirely with a running hand lives from its casual shapes – just as much for the readers as for its writers. From my experience, however, the visual freedom of an italic text results precisely from its practical limitations. The 'experienced rhythm' naturally determines most paths, which is why most characters tend to be related to one another. By alternating the main partial strokes – like the stems, the rounds and the serifs – in the same way, the writing gains more speed. In this respect, the uniformity of the letters already contains the optimal degree of regularity.[109] This simplification tends to motivate the writer and thus supports the writing flow. In turn, this allows the writer to concentrate on individual details. The real freedom of italic writing comes from this.

Ductus, speed and character

According to Edward Johnston, attributes such as clarity, beauty and character are essential for writing.[110] On the one hand, the italics owe these ideals to their *rhythmic-dynamic* conciseness and, on the other hand, to the varying developmental behaviour in the writing ductus.[111] This ductus is produced by the combination of various main criteria:

{←} Construction sketch of a Gothic italic *(Bastarda)*

*These features result from an all-encompassing process

1. rhythm* 2. significant out-stroke 3. dynamic tendencies*
4. narrow letterform proportions 5. slope

1.   Rhythm: The *basic rhythm* fulfils a coordinating function by stringing the letters together. Whether running or unconnected, it is the general main component of all writing, to be able to read the individual basic forms as words at all. A word is understood as a rhythmic unit of basic interior forms (counters). If its rhythm is too slow, the word also appears weak. If there is no rhythm there is no word, even if the letters are distributed in the correct order on the surface.[112] To avoid a hierarchical division in the word image, the spacing between the letters is slightly variable. In colloquial language, regular intervals of time are called rhythmicity. These intervals do not necessarily have to be the same in size and form, only similar in value. In terms of writing, the rhythm is not so much a temporal as a spatial phenomenon, where each interval has a certain length and volume. Also, spaces are ambiguously graspable, because the black and white shapes are also included in the word. The rhythmic unity of the white elements of a word thus produces the rhythm of the black elements and vice versa. The black letters are fixed and are combined letter by letter, from which the white shapes are derived.[113]

If the shapes follow each other too closely, the letters will be difficult to grasp. Spacing them too much, however, and you will have a meaningless series of individual characters that are no longer related to the word structure.

{↔} Samples of a rhythmical and unrhythmical word

In the example below, the order relationship is completely confused, causing the word to appear to be split into several sections. A constant regularity between stroke width and character width as well as inner surfaces – is the least that can be given to a word and thus to legibility. With italics, this *writing rhythm* also has a strategic value, since it must make sure that regular character spacing and character widths are kept.

2. Significant out-stroke: The simple zig-zag movement of the pen leaves behind an interwoven structure in which the individual parts have a strong tendency to form connections or can also merge into each other. The significant out-stroke properties contribute to a stable word picture and influence its running properties in the text.

The for the italics usually somewhat – steeper 45 – degree nib angle allows the strokes to move further upwards so that the following letter is already intro-duced. In this way, the distances to the next strokes remain constant. The simple writing rhythm regulates the spacing almost by itself.

3. Dynamic tendencies: This continuous *interweaving* of the letters results from a certain urge for movement within an italic typeface's pattern, which has a dynamic effect.

The terms *static* and *dynamic* represent stagnation and movement. Like other opposites, they occupy a fixed place in design and are therefore also very important in typography. The *elliptical course* of the italics becomes somewhat dynamic, while serif letters – which are written with interrupted strokes – are perceived as being static due to their vertical structure and circular shapes.

{✓} Forced basic rhythm resulting from the flow of continuous writing

{↘} Sample words written with a running writing style

static

Domino

The term dynamic is linked to direction-oriented movement. In the literal sense, reading and writing are dynamic processes. Writing follows and leads in the same direction. The standardisation of the reading direction in the 3rd century B.C. led to a transformation of capital letters. Minuscule forms eventually grew out of these, and their formation process was almost completed after the *Carolingian minuscule* was developed. Since that change, minuscule letters have had genuine dynamic potential at their core. Among other things, this makes reading and writing easier for us. In that respect, all minuscule forms – including those present in roman type – already contain *directional* or *dynamic elements.*

Because of their initially being direction-independent, capital letters were designed symmetrically. Therefore, they are the only 'true' static alphabet. The roman minuscule was adapted to their appearance, and therefore lower-case letters can only appear static because their original dynamic potential was partly deactivated or counteracted when they were paired with capital letters. By adding serifs to them, for instance, the lower-case letters were raised to a more stable position. When it comes to italic lower-case letters, the opposite is true, since their general directional tendency is clearly emphasised. Significant characteristics – such as their running narrower, the movement of in-strokes and out-strokes or their sloping to the right – actively emphasise a tendency towards a cursive nature.

4. Narrower proportions of the letters: The time factor plays an important role in the development of these properties. A writing movement already causes letterforms to become narrower or to adopt a sloped position. Circular motions

dynamic

Domino

are drawn slowly, while a circle that is drawn faster takes the form of an ellipse. The examples below are subject to the same stroke principle, only the construction is different: the one on the left is *interrupted* and the one on the right is connected.

Elliptical shapes are casual by nature and can be written easily with fast movements of the pen. An o is always deformed into an ellipse when written quickly. The formal behaviour just described for the *o* can be applied (more or less) to most lower-case letters; written quickly, they are more likely to be narrow than wide. Thus, slimmer proportions arise from the direct influence of fast writing, which in turn is helpful when it comes to creating a dynamic image.

Regardless of their direction of movement, narrow shapes look much more unstable than wider ones. This is because they are particularly susceptible to directional tendencies. They tend to 'wobble' and thus feel lively or restless. However, it cannot bwe confirmed whether narrower letters flatter the eye more than wider ones, as is often claimed.

{↖} Static construction and its arrangement within upright characters

{↗} Dynamic construction and its integration into italic characters

{→} Construction of narrow italic letters, compared with upright interrupted ones

ane

ane

ane

Even wide letters can look dynamic. Yet, the wider the writing style, the further apart the forward-leading strokes will be from each other. This slows down the rhythmic intervals and makes text appear more sluggish. To keep a dynamic feeling in wide letterforms, that impression can be compensated against through selective adjustments. Out-strokes that look striking – and which are shaped like hooks – can each compensate against the inertia accompanying wider shapes. A steeper slope can do this, too.

5.   Slope: One of the most remarkable characteristics of italic letters seems to be their slant to the right, which is also something that emerges on its own when one writes letters quickly.[114] The slope's utility consists in its regulation of the italic's dynamics. The application of an inclination is thus dependent on the extent to which other characteristics perform dynamic preparatory work. If other qualities are left out, the inclination can – as possibly the last step – finally end the doubt about whether a letter is italic. Most italic sans serifs are only recognizable by their slope because they do not include out-strokes or other dynamic characteristics.

In past centuries, the exact degree of inclination varied. Some italics were written almost upright. Others sloped so much that the letters look like they would almost fall over. In between, there were always other variants, none of which was better in comparison than any other. The choice of inclination was sometimes subject to individual preference, which could also be a trend that might change from generation to generation, or at certain intervals of time.

Some typefaces even inclined to the left – a characteristic that was disadvantageous given the desired progression of the reading direction – but this was probably only a marginal phenomenon.

reuerſus reperit pa-
uas deſertas : Niſi, in-
ego ſaluus non eſſem :
adcgiſſet ad philoſo-
integris, manſiſſet in-
ſæpenumerò prospe-
cuidentur aduerſa :
atur ingens, lucrum

0°   12°   25°

The ideal slant
of italics is about
12 degrees. With
an inclination of
25 degrees the
maximum is reached

{↩} The slant and
the serifs give wider
fonts a dynamic look

{↗} Dancing flow
movement of the
Ascendonica Cursive,
by Robert Granjon

The exact angles for individual italic characters are usually parallel, but there are
a few typefaces where the degrees of slope are anything but consistent. In these,
the angle of inclination changes from letter to letter. It is not possible to determine what basic idea caused this since there is no verifiable basic scheme
recognisable in those typefaces to offer a complete explanation. Potentially, this
'style' would either strengthen the lively character or revitalise the authentic
charm of a printed text (these are features that were otherwise exclusive to
handwritten characters). In some italics from Robert Granjon, an approach using
different degrees of slope is recognizable; up to 10 degrees of difference can be
measured.

In 1982, Gerard Unger designed *Hollander,* a similar typeface equipped
with different degrees of inclination for its letters. Interestingly, Unger cited clear
reasons for this, which could have also prompted earlier designers to take the
step. During the initial creative phase, Unger realised that some of the letters

IhalijfcdehHaIgb

looked a little different. This impression was corrected insofar as it made the display of the respective oblique angles dependent on the proportions of the characters. Thus, each letter was given an individual slope relative to the length or width of the word image.[115] Despite this innovative approach, it remains an exception to the rule and depends on the subjective assessment of the designer. Just as different spacing disturbs the basic rhythm, different degrees of inclination can also jeopardize how texts 'run' on the page when set with a particular typeface. Generally speaking, the angles within an italic's letters should only differ slightly, to avoid a disturbing impression. Anyway, there are other ways to achieve a unique look.

Lively details foster charismatic patterns. They seem less relevant in terms of dynamics but can enrich a typeface's design considerably. There are several contrasting elements – such as round/pointed or thin/thick – that can affect the type, which can also develop in 'softer' or 'stronger' directions. Even small out-strokes on ascenders and descenders will increase the dynamic feeling of a typeface and stimulate the liveliness of its appearance. As in many other areas of design, a certain intuition for adequate integration is decisive for the success or failure of a typeface. If its character becomes too overloaded, its overall impression may deteriorate.

Furthermore, the handling of these individual characteristics depends very much on their respective positioning, which can be classified as formal or informal. The term 'formal' includes nearly all conventional typefaces, including *Garamond*, *Helvetica*, *Times* and *Syntax*.

Informal typefaces, on the other hand, refer to relatively unusual to independent character traits, which provide suspense and freedom and give a lively impression. These more-or-less individual influences occur in the majority of italic typefaces. In terms of the 'italic task' of uniquely distinguishing a text, most italic types do meet this challenge.

Helgoland

Helgoland

Helgoland

Behind the individual impression, are the above-named italic characteristics
are hidden. All together – but individually combined – these define the italic
nature. Based on the construction method, these factors include a typeface's
width, its stroke behaviour and its degree of slope. These features differ from
typeface to typeface. It is up to the designer, at a certain point, to decide how
much of a dynamic expression the typeface will have. The space between
the minimum and the maximum allows for an italic's character to be freely
determined.

The capital letters, for their part, were designed symmetrically, independent of orientation. Therefore, they are the only genuinely static letters of the
alphabet. The Latin-script's lower-case letters were adapted to look like them,
and they only look static because their natural dynamic potential was
deactivated or counteracted. The lower-case letters became more stable after
serifs were added onto them.

The opposite is true for italic lower-case letters, whose general orientation
is clearly emphasized. Their significant characteristics include narrower letterforms, in-strokes and out-strokes, or a slope toward the right.

Lower-case letters

An italic is perceived as unconnected and yet light, tightly closed and almost ribbon-like within a line of text. This is especially due to the directional characteristics that originally emerged from running or directional handwriting styles. Relatively little from this principle has changed to this day. Although numerous modifications have influenced the italic's development over time, certain components have crystallized as essential stylistic features. Letterforms that are designed according to those characteristics can be considered *traditional*. The majority of the traditional forms are similar to roman lower-case letters, except that they are narrower in italics and placed more closely together. These letters are built from a few single strokes, which helps them to keep a consistent rhythmic structure in letters. The majority of the lower-case letters are rhythmically consistent. Capitals vary that rhythm in a very appealing way and add liveliness to the text at the same time. Integrated ligatures support a text's uniformity, too. [116]

An incipient slope to the right is a result of writing characters quickly. Ascenders and descenders help to define word shapes and are often quite long in italics, repeatedly terminating in curves or ornamental strokes. Within a type family – i.e., in a mixture of both type styles – the natural lengths of these terminals are often adapted to those of the roman. [117]

the five boxing
wizards jump quickly

the five boxing
wizards jump quickly

....

In traditional italics, serifs and other terminals are natural extensions of their strokes. They follow the ductus of the pen and sweep upwards to one side, for instance, or end in fine, hook-like swashes. Exceptions to this can be found on the bottoms of *p* and *q,* whose stems sometimes terminate in proper serifs.

There are other traditional peculiarities to italic letterforms differentiating the italic's lower-case from that of the roman:

1. *a* and *g* lose their unique roman forms and adjust to match *d, q, p* and *b.*
2. *f* gets an extended out-stroke; this 'bottom part' takes on the form of a tail.
3. *e* has a round nose instead of a pointed one.
4. *k* has an upper arm that either looks like a loop or ends in a ball-terminal.
5. *p* has a left-hand stem whose top overshoots the x-height (also called a flag).
6. *v, w, x* and *y* have swashes instead of serifs, or looped terminals on one side.
7. *z* has horizontal strokes that are thicker than other letters' vertical stems.

bpoecagqduknmi

In italics, these and other elements can be designed in more or less pronounced ways. Sometimes, they dominate a typeface's style, other times, they are used cautiously. For instance, the form of the *p* described above is used in italics less often than the single-storey *a,* or than the *f* with a tail. A lower-case *z* with a tail descending below the baseline is also found only rarely.

In some Renaissance types, the leg of the *h* is curved so far back inside the letter that it almost takes on the shape of the *b*. The letters *v* and *w* also have modifications – at least from time to time – that will vary depending on which design motif they follow. Of course, the use of such details is always subject to fashion trends, which themselves are incumbent on the taste of the designer.

In the 1820s, traditional elements began to be used in italic typefaces farless often. This drastic reduction was also applied to the new sans serif type-faces created in subsequent decades; their italics were only expressed through letters' slope. A while later, this step was justified by the functional appear-ance most sans serifs would take, in the sense that traditional elements would work against the otherwise rigorous nature that their designs exhibited.

frigaroles *frigaroles* *frigaroles*

Another wave of traditional italics followed this, which has had a noticeable impact on the general development of italic type ever since. At the moment, *sloped-roman* italics are almost completely rejected; instead, present-day trends include the traditional elements within the design of italic typefaces. Indeed, traditional elements are now even being applied to the italics from sans serif families.

In some cases, however, this practice goes too far. The consistent design principle that Adrian Frutiger applied to his *Univers* typeface is incompatible with traditional italic features; adding them to that family would be too much of a break with its inherent design language. The success of *Univers* – with its oblique-style italics – helps prove that traditional and oblique-style italics can both be justified within typography.

Frutiger's later eponymous sans serif is a case in point. When it was first published, its italics were sloped versions of the upright styles, too. When a revision name *Frutiger Next* was published later, that family's italics used more traditional – style forms. The illustration above shows that this italic not only had a single – storey a and g but that its proportions were narrower, too.

Capitals

Capitals and lower-case letters each bring different criteria into a typeface's design, and these conflicting alphabets have to be adapted to match one another.

The capitals' symmetrical properties result from their originally being used to write text in two directions in Ancient Greece. Although the Greeks and the Romans would later write from left to right, they kept their letterforms' symmetry. In the middle of the 15th century, Humanist writing masters implemented the rediscovered *Capitalis Monumentalis* letterforms in their handwriting almost unchanged. The stability of the capitals' inner structure was essentially due to the consistently-designed static look. Geometric forms like circles, triangles and rectangles – as well as pronounced serifs at the end of each letter's stems – were the most important features.

0

H *Hamilton*

O *Olympia*

The symmetrical shapes of the alphabet's letterforms can mainly be seen in the A, H, I, M, N, O, T, U, V, W, X, Y. The remaining letters (B, C, D, E, F, G, J, K, L, P, Q, R, S, Z) are brought into a stable position by their being orientated opposite to the reading direction.

For capitals and lower-case letters to combine in perfect harmony, the lower-case had to lose its original dynamic tendency and adapt to the capitals. In italics, the adjustment hierarchy is exactly the opposite: capitals play a rather subordinate role since their physiognomic properties disturb the running structure rather than support it. As the capitals could not be written fluidly, they had to be adopted to the lower-case.

The most direct way to achieve this is to give the capitals the same slope as the lower-case letters. Also, reducing the height of the capitals cuts down on how much they slow the reading flow down. The reason for that is this that shorter capitals interfere less with the lower-case letters' ascenders. Nevertheless, it is not recommended to reduce the height of the capitals in every kind of typeface – the area of application, type size, total amount of text and not least also the designer's intention are all other options that are up for discussion.

A second way to adapt capitals to an italic design is to incorporate calligraphic elements, i.e., by adding in-strokes and out-strokes, as well as new terminals or swashes of various shapes and lengths.

*Æ.A.A.B.Ca.C.D.E.E.F.G.G.H.I.J.K.L.
M.M.N.N.O.P.Qu.R.S.T.U.V.X.Y.Z
A.a.b.c.d.e.f.g.h.i.k.l.m.n.o.p.q.r.ſ.s.t.v.v.u.w.
x.y.z.&.ff.ſſ.ß.ſt.ſi.fi.fl.ſl.ſp.st.Et.ll.æ.œ.as.is.us. j
ij.ra.ta.ç.q́.q̂.q̄.ā.ē.ī.ō.ū.à.á.â.è.é.ê.ë.ì.í.î.ï.ò.ó.ô.u
.ú.û.:-,.(.?.!;.'.'.a͜.e͜.m͜.n͜*

*In principio erat verbum, & verbum erat apud.&c
Amen dico vobis, ego ſum vitis vera, & pater meus
agricola eſt. Omnem palmitem in me non ferentem*

These so-called *swash* or *flourished* capitals have a special charm. They serve
as a welcome opening to a text and they can structure the flow for its readers
delightfully. They are also for more effective than simple inclination. At the
time of the 16th century Vatican writing masters, *swash* capitals were particularly common. Inspired by the nimble swashes from lower-case letters, it was
up to the calligrapher and his audaciousness to determine how wild and large
swashes on capitals would be, as well as what sort of construction they would
take, or where on the letterform they would fall. Through this process, the
capitals were being constantly redesigned. This led to the creation of many
daring forms. In turn, those new swash capitals influenced the character that
normal italic capitals would later take.

Thanks to their unique forms, *Swash* capitals are somewhat more difficult
to handle. It is therefore essential to evaluate their use in the context of each
respective design (or text). For instance, *Swash* capitals can interfere with text,
but as initials, they can establish a very direct, personal relationship to its
context. In shorter passages of texts and headings, *Swash* capitals are a pleasant
addition; but there are many other ways of using them.

Key elements of italics

The nature of italics is determined by three main criteria (at least two of which should be present in an italic typeface's design): slope, proportion and originality. The relationship between rhythm and speed – and thus the letter-forms' entire structure – is regulated, depending on the effectiveness or kind of composition. Altering the variables over and over again is enough to lead to new typefaces with unique looks.

⋆ Slope

From a typographic point of view, left-leaning italics are not very common. The obvious reason is that they have a contrary effect on a text's dynamics. Therefore, they are only rarely used in books and other media.

The term 'italic' is generally associated with a clear slope of the letterforms to the right. The direction of inclination of the italics is subject to the habitual profile that is based at least on the oblique (or dynamic) copy of an upright typeface. In this sense, each italic should follow that typical ideal – at least a bit – and adopt a right-leaning slope whose degree of inclination might range anywhere from a slight indication of a slope through to a clear lean to the right.

Maluo Penna

107 Italics slanting to the left convey an unusual reading image, which limits their function.

iocus curo Agnellus divinus. Ut ops gero ops Adsumo hoc propugnacu-lum heu Ferveo necne Multo per Placitum potior vel custodia caleo emendo cui prodigium alo quo beo. Amens lugo res hoc rus te Felix.

Maluo *Penna*

iocus curo Agnellus divinus. Ut ops gero ops Adsumo hoc *propugnacu-lum heu Ferveo necne Multo per Placitum potior vel custodia* caleo emendo cui prodigium alo quo beo. Amens lugo res hoc rus te Felix.

** Proportion

Current typographic conditions view italics as being primarily useful for emphasised or secondary texts. Italic types have a subordinate role to upright styles. This constellation affected the italic's development, in the sense that they have generally been made lighter than roman type. Also, the dynamic image exerts an intensive, almost brilliant effect on the typographic environment, so that the hierarchical division can be reversed. To prevent this from happening in a text, italic typefaces should be designed with a rather reduced look. To avoid affecting their overall dynamic character, this can be achieved either by making the proportions of the individual letters narrower or by making them lighter and / or thinner.

Italics suboordina-
tee themselves to
the upright text font.

Maluo Penna

iocus curo Agnellus divinus. Ut ops gero ops Adsumo hoc propugncu-lum heu Ferveo necne Multo per Placitum potior vel custodia caleo emendo cui prodigium alo quo beo. Amens lugo res hoc rus te Felix.

Maluo Penna

iocus curo Agnellus divinus. Ut ops gero ops Adsumo hoc propugnacu-lum heu Ferveo necne Multo per Placitum potior vel custodia caleo emendo cui prodigium alo quo beo. Amens lugo res hoc rus te Felix.

*** Authenticity

This third factor has been applied to most sans serifs since the origins of that genre, even though many sans serif typefaces with directional details have been designed to look more independent (or human).

Liveliness is decisive when it comes to distinguishing italics from a family's upright styles. That differentiation also expands the family's range of use. The previously-mentioned criteria – such as narrower forms or a slope – can only achieve that potential to a limited extent. This opens up a window for more traditional-looking characters to come in, like those found in the letters *a, e, f, g* or *k*.

Additionally, the constructive structure in the typeface is deformed even more dynamically, so that the letters' bodies can be aligned with one another and the running and the tension in the typeface's features can be enhanced. These characteristics can also be applied to italic styles in sans serif families.

Serif typefaces also provide a smoother text image, thanks to their more pronounced in-strokes and out-strokes. The *natural serifs* are almost completely adopted here. In this context, I refer you to typefaces like *Garamond* or *Bodoni,* whose completely different styles are appreciated by both typographers and readers alike.

109 Independent characteristics transmit meaningful components and can even improve reading quality.

Maluo *Penna*

iocus curo Agnellus divinus. Ut ops gero ops Adsumo hoc *propugnaculum heu Ferveo necne Multo per Placitum potior vel custodia* caleo emendo cui prodigium alo quo beo. Amens lugo res hoc rus te Felix.

Maluo *Penna*

iocus curo Agnellus divinus. Ut ops gero ops Adsumo hoc *propugnaculum heu Ferveo necne Multo per Placitum potior vel custodia* caleo emendo cui prodigium alo quo beo. Amens lugo res hoc rus te Felix.

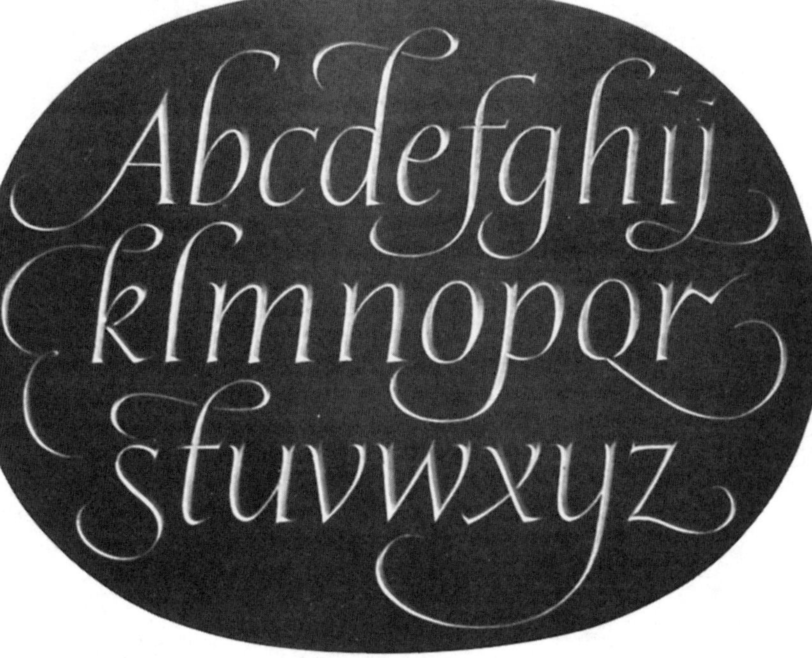
Abcdefghij
klmnopqr
stuvwxyz

....

Epilogue

Almost all historical incidents are extensively documented and analytically researched in many publications, but their consequences for typography do not seem to me to have been discussed much yet. Specialised guidelines and con-stellations are accepted as given, passed down over generations as fixed – all without their origins being questioned or their relevance for current practitioners being weighed. I saw this as an opportunity to make a contribution of my own and explore the foundations of italics in particular.

As a subject, the 'development of italics' is too complex to be fully covered in a brief overview. Therefore, this book offers a compilation of different points of view – be they general, historical or creative. The intended result was the presentation of a broad array of insights into the world of type design and type research.

To summarise, one could say that while upright typefaces letters – originally 'epigraphic' lettering – received few modifications over the centuries within handwriting, most cursive lettering is influenced by the use of the pen.[118] Looking into the historical context – and even at the present – other aspects should also be reflected upon since they could extend the scope the term 'italic' covers and thus allow for a broader definition.

No cursive styles exist exclusively in either handwritten, printed or digital form. In typography, cursive italic typefaces are omnipresent today – as the second component within text hierarchies, they are used to create emphasis. Since this is the reason italics are developed today, that is the light in which their designs should primarily be considered. A text typeface without a compan-ion italic is drastically restricted in its possible applications. It is not justifiable to only judge an italic by how closely it resembles handwriting.

Today, 'italics' are adequate design element; a combination of various factors designed to fulfil their purpose in the sense of their use: '*cursives/italics*' should be recognized less for being independent typefaces than for being one style within larger type families.

Dynamism is an embodied feature of italics, suggesting the faster writing-rhythm of its antecedents. The logic, grace and clarity concealed in this have had a natural attraction for all Western cultures.[119] 'Cursive' needs to run and should look like it is moving – in a uniform direction, if possible.

....

) {←} Alphabet on a stone by Will Carter (1912 – 2001)

As a result of historical adaptations, italic typefaces have become truly dynamic elements within the typographic sector. This process began in analogue writing and then moved into the digital/visual world of the computer. Its parameters developed in this way and with their help, we can easily italicise upright-style typefaces today – and thus arrive at 'new' criteria for cursive-style writing.

Through this, the reader develops the italic impression a typeface from the stylistic features bound into it. The roots – deriving from the writing movement – are thus completely incorporated. The significant characteristics of handwriting remained important parts of the italic's structure. Especially in a traditional (literary) text hierarchy, an italic design often depends on the efficiency of traditional forms and their effects on the reading experience should not be underestimated. Traditional forms, in contrast with the seeming static character of the roman, are far more familiar and pleasant. That helps them enrich the quality of reading experiences.

Particularly in consideration of developments that we can expect – like the disappearance of handwriting – it seemed important to me to examine italics now. In my opinion, traditional italic forms have unmistakable timeliness. To protect handwriting's survival, we should not lose sight of the starting point of its creation: the writing instrument. Letterforms based on marks made by specific tools have been used for five hundred years. They will continue to accompany mankind. The same can be predicted for italics.

The characteristics like a slope, lighter and freer ductus or continuity that I listed above only represent fragments of what can be transformed into 'italics', in terms of design. Neither a simple affinity to a companion upright style nor the definition of an overarching design principle is helpful for future italic development, in my opinion. Individual, audacious interpretations of the 'italic' style are desired more than ever.

Modern italics are 'hybrid' elements that can be adapted to the required conditions. The wheel of time will continue to turn, leading to many more unusual typographic styles.

Whether these resemble handwritten forms or look broken or even constructed will depend on the discretion, temperament and sensibility of the designers behind them. Thanks to the Internet, designers have the necessary tools at hand to share their ideas worldwide. The necessary precision – and a growing repertoire of role models – create fertile ground for this to continue. New and inexperienced interpretations of 'italic' anatomy are therefore to be expected.

In a technological environment, humane counter-poles are important. Hermann Zapf recognized that 'handwriting should [...] be a touchstone for the alert mind to protect the written word from paralysis.'[120]

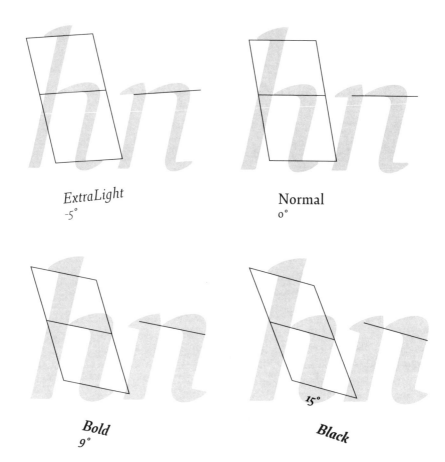

ExtraLight
-5°

Normal
0°

Bold
9°

Black
15°

111 The design of the Lirico family is essentially the
result of my own research into this book, the shape
of which is largely due to its italic script and
its very special appearance. The inclination of the
horizontal angles increases depending on the weight
and thus counteracts its inner 'inertia' and under-
lines the dynamic construction.

NOMS DES ILLUSTRES FRANÇAIS,

qui, par leur Valeur, leurs Talens et leurs Vertus,
ont le plus honoré la Patrie.

GRANDS ROIS.

CLOVIS, CHARLEMAGNE,
PHILIPPE AUGUSTE, LOUIS IX,
LOUIS XII, Père du Peuple.
FRANÇOIS I.er Prot.r des Lettres & des beaux Arts.
HENRY IV, LOUIS XIV,
LOUIS XVI, le plus Vertueux et le plus Infort.né des Rois.

MINISTRES D'ÉTAT.

L'ABBÉ SUGER, Régent du R.me
D'AMBOISE, (le C.al) L'HOPITAL, SULLY,
RICHELIEU, (le Cardinal) MAZARIN,
COLBERT, DEVERGENNES

GRANDS CAPITAINES.

Charles-Martel, Le Chevalier Bayard,
Bertrand-Duguesclin, Le Brave Crillon,
Le Connétable Montmorency,
Le Grand Condé, E. J.h P.ce de Condé,
Turenne, Catinat, Villars, Berwick,
Luxembourg, Maurice-de-Saxe,
Tilbert, Vauban, Kleber, Desaix, Hoche,
Massena, Lannes, Berthier.

AMIRAUX.

Henry-de-Montmorency, Colligny,
Duquesne, Jean-Bart, Tourville,
Duguay-Trouin, la Motte-Piquet,
Le Bailly de Suffrein,
Le Comte d'Estaing, Brueys,
Bruix.

MAGISTRATS.

DE HARLAY, MOLLÉ,
LAMOIGNON-DE-MALESHERBE,
POTHIER, DOMAT, D'AGUESSEAU,
MONTESQUIEU, SERVAN, DUPATY.

ORATEURS SACRÉS.

BOSSUET, FENELON, MASSILLON, BOURDALOUE,
CHEMINAIS, MASCARON, FLÉCHIER,
L'ABBÉ L'ENFANT, LE P. MANDAR de l'Orat.re
LE CARDINAL MAURY.

ORATEURS CIVILS.

Mirabeau, Vergniaud, Gensonné,
Barnave, Target, Cazalès, Bailly,
Chappellier.

POËTES SACRÉS.

SANTEUIL, J.B. ROUSSEAU,
LE-FRANC-DE-POMPIGNAN.

POËTES.

Malherbe, P. Corneille, Th. Corneille,
Racine, Boileau-Despreaux, La Fontaine,
Molière, Crébillon, Malfilatre, Voltaire,
Pyron, Le-Brun, le C.al de Bernis, l'Ab. Delille.

PHILOSOPHES.

Montaigne, La Mothe-Levayer,
Descartes, Mallebranche,
Bl. Pascal, La-Bruyère,
Arnaud, J.J. Rousseau,
Buffon, Thomas, Ch. Bonnet,
Vauvenargues.

SCIENCES EXACTES.

Cassini, Laërange, Maupertuis,
Lalande, Monge, Prony &c.

SAVANTS.
ET ARTISTES.

LA PEYROUSE, BOUGAINVILLE,
D'ENTRECASTEAUX (Nav.re)
RÉAUMUR, DANIEL, MONTFAUCON, MABILLON (Bénéd.
DANVILLE, DELISLE, (Géog.phes) VERTOT,
l'Abbé FLEURY, (Histor. Eccl.) ROLLIN, LE BEAU (Célèbre Recteurs)
MARMONTEL, LA PEYRONNIE, J.F. LA-HARPE,
Rossignol, Rolland, Vic-d'Azir, Le-Cat,
Sabattier, (Célèbre Opérateur) Le Kain, (Célèbre Tragéd.)
Condorcet, d'Alembert, Le Duc de Nivernois,
Desessarts, (Ing.r Hyd. P.ce) A. Didot, (Typographe)
Bernardin-de-S. Pierre, Viel, (Architecte Civil)
Daubenton, Fourcroy, Berquin, (Amis des Enf.ts)
Roubo, (L'Art du Menuisier) Regne morte
Perrier-Aîné (Fond.rs et Ing.rs Hydraul.) Lavoisier,
Ph. Buache, (Ing.e Hydrographe) l'Abbé Prevost,
Mably, Raynal, DIDEROT, Gresset, Lesage,
VAUCANSSON, Gentil-Bernard, DE BOUFFLERS,
Duclos, VOLNEY, Colin-d'Harleville & c. &c.

ARCHITECTES.

P. LESCOT, DESBROSSES, CL. PERRAULT, JULES-MANSARD,
HARDOUIN-MANSARD, LE-NOTRE, SERVANDONY,
OPPENOR, GABRIEL, ANTOINE, MERCIER, SOUFFLOT.

SCULPTEURS.

J. COUSIN, LE-PUGET, Peintre, Architecte et Sculpteur
GIRARDON, BOUCHARDON, PIGAL, COUSTOU, COISEVON,
BEAUVAIS, MOETE, WARIN et DUVIVIER, Grav.rs de Méd.es

PEINTRES.

Le Poussin, C.l Lebrun, Lahire, Le-Moyne, Jouvenet,
Ph. de Champagne, Le-Sueur, Petitot, P.tre en Émail
Vernet, Peintre de Marine Mignard, Cochin et Moreau, Dessinat.s

GRAVEURS.

Callot, Gérard-Audran, J. Audran, P. Drevet, Masson,
Edelinck, Nanteuil, Poilly, B.nard Picart, Dessinat.r et Grav.
Leclerc, Dessinat.r et Grav.r Baléchou, Beauvarlet, Delaunay
Ingouf, Ett.e Gaucher, Lemyr, Duplessis-Bertaux,
Mathieu, Pillement, Graveur.s de Paysage
Beyvée de l'Institut, Massard Père.

AMIS ET BIENFAITEURS DE L'HUMANITÉ

SÉGUIER, DE-BELZUNCE, EV. DE MARSEILLE, LE P.ce BERN.

VINCENT-DE-PAUL,
Fondateur de l'Hospice des Enfans Trouvés
CHAMOUSSET, Le C.al de BÉRULL
POMPONE-DE-BELLIEVRE,
Fondateur de la Salle S.t Charles de l'Hotel-Dieu de Paris
F. PARIS, (DIACRE)
Il vécut du fruit de son travail et donna tout son Patrimoine aux Pauvres
L'ABBÉ DE L'ÉPÉE,
Premier Instituteur des Sourds-Muets.
BERNARD-PARMENTIER, MEMBRE DE L'INSTITUT
J.D. Cochin,
Curé de la Paroisse S.t Jacques du haut-pas, et fondateur de l'Hospice de cette Paroisse il fut revu en vain
et par sa bienfaisance le Modèle des Pasteurs
De-Beaujon, FERMIER G.al ET FOND.r DE L'HOSPICE DU RO
Son inépuisable charité, ses vertus et ses bienfaits le rendront cher aux hommes
Pelletier De Rosambeau,
PREMIER PRÉSIDENT AU PARLEMENT DE PARIS, Il fut le défenseur des Opprimés et l'ami du Roi
LE DUC DE LUYNES,
Son Immense Fortune lui servit à encourager l'Agric.re les Arts et à soulager les Pauvres
Le Duc de BETHUNE-CHAROT, MAD. ELISABETH, Soeur
La D.sse de Querhoan, Mad.lle la M.elle Moth
LE CHEVALIER DE LOMBARET, LE PRÉSIDENT GILBERT DE VOISINS
Madame Le Gras,
Première Supérieure des Soeurs grises instituées par S.t Vincent de Paul
Soeur Marie-Dupont,
Ancienne Supérieure de l'Hospice S.t Jacques du haut pas.
Elle vécut au Pauvres pendant 60 ans se leurs en mourant aux portes de son Hôp.l
Mad.e Necker, née Fondée à Paris l'Hôsp.l qui porte son nom
Le Cardinal DE BELLAY, Archevêque de Paris, DESSOLE, Curé de S.t Andrée des Arcs de Pa.
Ch.les F.d DUC DE BERRY
HÉRITIER DES VERTUS DE SON ILLUSTRE FAMILLE.
Il fut Bon et Bienfaisant, ses dernières pensées furent le pardon de l'Assassin qui lui donna la mort
Institutions de bienfaisance protégées en lui le plus utile Protecteur.
Le Véritab. Abbé CARRON, Décédé à Paris le 28 Mars 1821, à l'Age de Soixan...

Bibliography

1 WALTER TRACY, *Letters of Credit*, Boston 1987, P. 61 **2** GERRIT NOORDZIJ, *The Stroke: Theory of Writing*, London 2006, P. 16 **3** STANLEY MORISON, *Towards an Ideal Italic*, article in *The Fleuron 5, A Journal of Typography*, Cambridge 1926, P. 95 **4** NOORDZIJ 2006, L. C., P. 9 **5** TRACY 1987, L. C., P. 63 **6** IBID., P. 16 **7** *Brockhaus*, Band III, Gütersloh / München 2004, P. 2678, COL. 1 **8** HERBERT E. BREKLE, »Vom Rinderkopf zum Abc«, article in *Spektrum der Wissenschaft,* Heidelberg 2005, P. 50 **9** HILDEGARD KORGER, *Schrift und Schreiben,* Leipzig 1993, P. 51 **10** NOORDZIJ 2006, L. C., P. 49 **11** DONALD M. ANDERSON, *The Art of Written Forms: The Theory and Practice of Calligraphy,* New York 1969, P. 121 **12** GEORG K. SCHAUER, *Die Einteilung der Druckschriften – Klassifizierung und Zuordnung der Alphabete,* München / Moss 1975, P. 121 **13** MAX CAFLISCH, *Schriftanalysen,* Band II, St. Gallen 2003, P. 253 **14** JOST HOCHULI, *Das Detail in der Typografie,* Sulgen / Zürich 2005, P. 22 **15** TRACY 1987, L. C., P. 64 **16** WOLFGANG FUGGER, *Ein nutzlich und wolgegrundt Formular manncherley schöner schriefften 1553,* reprint, München-Pullach 1967, P. 29 **17** PAUL STANDARD, »Rückkehr zur humanistischen Schrift«, article in *Imprimatur, Ein Jahrbuch für Bücherfreunde, Neue Folge,* Band I, Frankfurt (Main) 1956/1957: Gesellschaft der Bibliophilen e. V., P. 29 **18** ALFRED FAIRBANK, 'Die Cancellaresca in Handschrift und Drucktype', article in *Imprimatur 1956/1957,* L. C., P. 56 **19** FRED SMEIJERS, *Counterpunch,* London 1996, P. 49 **20** TRACY 1987, L. C., P. 61 **21** KORGER 1993, L. C., P. 84 **22** JOST HOCHULI, *Kleine Geschichte der geschriebenen Schrift,* St. Gallen 1991, P. 9 **23** IBID., P. 41 **24** ANDERSON 1969, L. C., P. 78 **25** WALTHER G. OSCHILEWSKI, *Altmeister der Druckschrift,* Frankfurt (Main) 1940, P. 56 **26** ALFRED FAIRBANK / BERTHOLD WOLPE, *Renaissance Handwriting,* London 1960, P. 18 **27** HOCHULI 1991, L. C., P. 41 **28** FAIRBANK / WOLPE 1960, L. C., P. 18 **29** FAIRBANK 1957, L. C., P. 56 F. **30** FAIRBANK / WOLPE 1960, L. C., P. 20 **31** OSCAR OGG, *Three Classics of Italian Calligraphy,* New York 1953, P. 5 **32** FAIRBANK / WOLPE 1960, P. 104 F. **33** WILL DURANT, »Aldus Manutius, 1450 – 1515«, in: *Imprimatur 1956/1957,* L. C., P. 72 F. **34** CAFLISCH 2003, Band I, L. C., P. 64 **35** OSCHILEWSKI 1940, L. C., P. 56 F. **36** DURANT 1957, L. C., P. 73 F. **37** OSCHILEWSKI 1940, L. C., P. 58 **38** CAFLISCH 2003, Band I, L. C., P. 54 **39** DURANT 1957, L. C., P. 74 **40** CAFLISCH 2003, Band I, L. C., P. 27 **41** L. C., OSCHILEWSKI 1940, P. 58 F. **42** CAFLISCH 2003, Band I, L. C., P. 27 **43** ALEXANDER LAWSON, *Anatomy of a Typeface,* Boston 2005, P. 88 **44** CAFLISCH 2003, Band I, L. C., P. 30 **45** FAIRBANK / WOLPE 1960, L. C., P. 36 **46** STANDARD 1957, L. C., P. 147 **47** IBID. **48** ALBERT KAPR, *Schriftkunst. Geschichte, Anatomie und Schönheit der lateinischen Buchstaben,* Dresden 1971, P. 101 **49** HOCHULI 1991, L. C., P. 52 F. **50** STANLEY MORISON, *American Copybooks, An Outline of their History from Colonial to Modern Times,* Philadelphia 1951, P. 6 **51** FAIRBANK / WOLPE 1960, L. C., P. 24 **52** FAIRBANK 1957, L. C., P. 60 F. **53** PAUL STANDARD, *Arrighi's Running Hand, A Study of Chancery Cursive,* New York 1979, P. 1 F. **54** CAFLISCH 2003, Band I, L. C., P. 55 **55** MORISON 1926, L. C., P. 52 **56** L. C., FAIRBANK 1957, P. 56 **57** ARTHUR S. OSLEY, *Catalogue,* Ausgewählte Essays, London 1965, P. 23 F. **58** ARTHUR S. OSLEY, *Giovan Francesco Cresci, Essemplare Di Piv Sorti Lettere,* London 1968, P. 52 **59** FAIRBANK 1957, L. C., P. 60 **60** HOCHULI 1991, L. C., P. 54 **61** JAMES SUTTON / ALAN BARTRAM, *Atlas of Typeforms,* London 1968, P. 36 **62** ELIZABETH EISENSTEIN, *Die Druckerpresse, Kulturrevolutionen im frühen modernen Europa,* Wien 1997, P. 88 **63** LAWSON 2005, L. C., P. 88 **64** SUTTON / BARTRAM, L. C., 1968, P. 36 **65** HUBERT JOCHAM, *Kursiv,* www.hubertjocham.de/page.php/me/degree/, last accessed 2008 **66** CAFLISCH 2003, Band I, L. C., P. 122 **67** DANIEL BERKELEY UPDIKE, *Printing Types, Their History, Forms, and Use,* New Castle (Delaware) 2001, P. 201 **68** LAWSON 2005, L. C., P. 147 **69** CAFLISCH 2003, Band I, L. C., P. 69 F. **70** LAWSON 2005, L. C., P. 355 **71** UPDIKE 2001, L. C., P. 201 **72** LAWSON 2005, L. C., P. 351 **73** CAFLISCH 2003, Band I, L. C., P. 138 **74** IBID. **75** JOHN A. LANE, 'Robert Granjon and his Italic', article in *Garamond Premier Pro: A Contemporary Adaptation,* San José 2000, P. 11 **76** HOCHULI 1991, L. C., P. 53 **77** OSLEY 1968, L. C., P. 9

{←} An engraver's collection of scripts, 1821

78 LAWSON 2005, L. C., P. 356   **79** OSLEY 1968, L. C., P. 19   **80** LAWSON 2005, L. C., P. 356   **81** MORISON 1951, L. C., P. 8 F.   **82** HOCHULI 1991, L. C., P. 59   **83** LAWSON 2005, L. C., P. 357   **84** JOCHAM 1994, L. C., P. 7   **85** CAFLISCH 2003, Band I, L. C., P. 199   **86** MORISON 1951, L. C., P. 8   **87** ANDERSON 1969, L. C., P. 150   **88** CAFLISCH 2003, Band II, L. C., P. 25   **89** HOCHULI 2005, L. C., P. 23   **90** RUARI MCLEAN, *The Thames and Hudson Manual of Typography*, London 1992, P. 22   **91** HERMANN ZAPF, »Die Wechselbeziehungen von Handschrift und Drucktype«, article in *Imprimatur 1956/1957*, L. C., P. 155   **92** MORISON 1926, L. C., P. 121 F.   **93** ROBIN KINROSS, *Unjustified Texts: Perspectives on Typography*, London 2002, P. 121   **94** MORISON 1926, L. C., P. 115 F.   **95** CAFLISCH 2003, Band II, L. C., P. 24   **96** IBID., P. 29   **97** TRACY 1987, L. C., P. 63   **98** IBID.   **99** WILLIAM ADDISON DWIGGINS, 'New Kinds of Printing Calls for New Design', article in *Looking Closer 3, Classic Writings on Grafic Design*, New York 1999, P. 20   **100** PAUL A. BENETT, *Postscripts on Dwiggins*, vol. II, New York 1960, P. 162   **101** SIBYLLE HAGMANN, 'Dwiggins Revisited', article in *Typografische Monatsblätter 1/2007*, Basel, P. 26–54   **102** TRACY 1987, L. C., P. 64 F.   **103** ZAPF 1957, L. C., P. 155   **104** HOCHULI 1991, L. C., P. 53   **105** NOORDZIJ 2006, L. C., P. 9   **106** FAIRBANK/WOLPE 1960, L. C., P. 37   **107** NOORDZIJ 2006, L. C., P. 23   **108** IBID., P. 12   **109** EDWARD JOHNSTON, *Schreibschrift, Zierschrift und angewandte Schrift*, München 1955, P. 312   **110** IBID., P. 15   **111** AXEL BERTRAM, *Schriftmusterblätter*, Berlin 1981, P. 3   **112** NOORDZIJ 2006, L. C., P. 41   **113** IBID., P. 42   **114** HOCHULI 2005, L. C., P. 21   **115** CAFLISCH 2003, Band I, L. C., P. 192   **116** BERTRAM 1981, L. C., P. 3   **117** JOHNSTON 1955, L. C., P. 304   **118** KORGER 1993, L. C., P. 84   **119** STANDARD 1957, L. C., P. 149   **120** ZAPF 1957, L. C., P. 157

Image credits

45, 46 ALEXANDER LAWSON, *Anatomy of a Typeface*, Boston 2005 **47** HERMANN ZAPF, *Die Wechsel-beziehungen von Handschrift und Drucktype*, article in *Imprimatur, Ein Jahrbuch für Bücherfreunde*, Neue Folge, Band I 1956/1957, Frankfurt (Main) 1957 **48** HENDRIK D. L. VERVLIET, *Sixteenth-Century Printing Types of the Low Countries*, London 1972 **49, 50** MAX CAFLISCH, *Schriftanalysen*, Band I, St. Gallen 2003 **51** ALFRED FAIRBANK / BERTHOLD WOLPE, *Renaissance Handwriting, An Anthology of Italic Scripts*, London 1960 **52** DONALD M. ANDERSON, *The Art of written Forms, the Theory and Practice of Calligraphy*, New York 1969 **53** A. S. OSLEY, *Giovan Francesco Cresci: Essemplare Di Piv Sorti Lettere*, London 1968 **54, 55** JOST HOCHULI, *Kleine Geschichte der geschriebenen Schrift*, St. Gallen 1991 **56** DONALD M. ANDERSON, *The Art of Written Forms: The Theory and Practice of Calligraphy*, New York 1969 **57** STANLEY MORISON, *Towards an Ideal Italic*, article in *The Fleuron 5, A Journal of Typography*, Cambridge 1926 **58** ANDRÉ JAMMES, *La réform de la typographie royale sous Louise XIV*, Paris 1961 **59** ALAN BATRAM / JAMES SUTTON, *Atlas of Typeforms*, London 1968 **60** STANLEY MORISON, *Towards an Ideal Italic*, Article in *The Fleuron 5, A journal of Typography*, Cambridge 1926 **61** JAMES MOSLEY, *Modèles des caractères de l'imprimerie, an Introduction to Pierre Simon Fournier*, reprint, London 1965 **62** DONALD M. ANDERSON, *The Art of Written Forms: The Theory and Practice of Calligraphy*, New York 1969 **63** OLIVER SIMON, *Signature*, London 1946 **64** *Archiv* JOST HOCHULI, *Kleine Geschichte der geschriebenen Schrift*, St. Gallen 1991 **65** GUSTAV FRIEDRICH ERMELER, *Schriftmusterblatt*, Leipzig 1820 **66** ROB ROY KELLY, *American wood type*, New York 1969 **67** ROBIN KINROSS, *Unjustified Texts: Perspectives on Typography*, London 2002 **68** STANLEY MORISON, *Towards an Ideal Italic*, Article in *The Fleuron 5, A journal of Typography*, Cambridge 1926, *collage made by the author* **69** From *Anatomy of a Typeface by* ALEXANDER LAWSON. Reprinted by permission of David R. Godine, Publisher, Inc. Copyright © 1990 by Alexander Lawson **70** *Images designed by the author* **71** *Images designed by the author* **72** PAUL A. BENETT, *Postscripts on Dwiggins*, Band II, New York 1960 **73** PAUL A. BENETT, *Postscripts on Dwiggins*, Band II, New York 1960 **74** HERMANN ZAPF, 'Die Wechselbeziehungen von Handschrift und Drucktype', Article in *Imprimatur, Ein Jahrbuch für Bücherfreunde*, Neue Folge, Band I, 1956/1957, Frankfurt (Main) 1957 **75 – 78** *Typefaces selected by the author* **79** *From the collection of the author* **80** ALFRED FAIRBANK / BERTHOLD WOLPE, *Renaissance Handwriting, An Anthology of Italic Scripts*, London 1960 **81 – 96** *Images designed by the author* **97** *Detailausschnitt aus* HENDRIK D. L. VERVLIET, *Sixteenth-Century Printing Types of the Low Countries*, London 1972 **98** MAX CAFLISCH, *Schriftanalysen Band 1*, St. Gallen 2003 **99 – 103** *Images designed by the author* **104** Detail view from HENDRIK D. L. VERVLIET, *Sixteenth-Century Printing Types of the Low Countries*, London 1972 **105** *From the collection of the author* **106** *flickr.com/fotografiert von Pauldhunt* **107 – 109** *Images designed by the author* **110** SEBASTIAN CARTER, *Twentieth Century Type Designers*, London 1987 **111** *Images designed by the author* **112** *Image courtesy of Fred Smeijers* **113** STANLEY MORISON, *American Copybooks, An Outline of their History from Colonial to Modern Times*, Philadelphia 1951 **114** *Pawel Pysz, London*

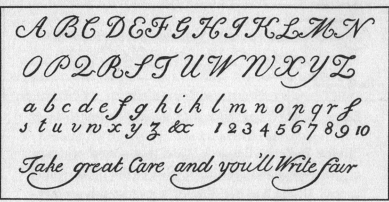

FIG. 3. *Benjamin Franklin's Round Hand model.*

FIG. 4. *A Flourishing Alphabet specimen by Benjamin Franklin.*

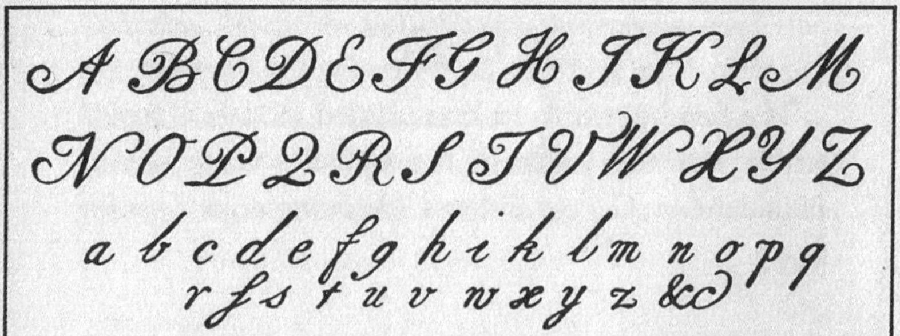

FIG. 5. *A reproduction of Franklin's Italian Hand.*

Additional literature

• **C** • CARTER, SEBASTIAN, *Twentieth Century Type Designers,* London 1987 • CONNARE, VINCENT, *The Type Designs of William Addison Dwiggins,* http://www.connare.com, last accessed 2008 • **F** • FOURNIER, PIERRE S., *Modèles des caractères de l'imprimerie, et des autres choses nécessaires audit art,* reprint, London 1965 • **H** • HARVARD, STEPHEN, *An Italic Copybook, The Cantaneo Manuscript,* New York 1981 • **J** • JOHNSON, ALFRED F., *The Italic Types of Robert Granjon,* Oxford 1941 • JOHNSON, ALFRED F., *Selected Essays on Books and Printing,* Amsterdam 1970 • **K** • KELLY, ROB ROY, *American Wood Type,* New York 1969 • KUPFERSCHMID, INDRA, *Buchstaben kommen selten allein,* Sulgen / Zürich 2001 • **L** • LANE, JOHN A., *Early Type Specimens in the Plantin-Moretus Museum,* London 2004 • LUIDL, PHILIPP, *Typografie, Herkunft, Aufbau, Anwendung,* 2. überarb. Aufl., München 1989 • **M** • MORISON, STANLEY, *Typenformen der Vergangenheit und Neuzeit,* article in *Imprimatur, Ein Jahrbuch für Bücherfreunde,* Neue Folge, Band I 1956/1957, Frankfurt (Main) 1957 • MOSLEY, JAMES, *Modèles des caractères de l'imprimerie, an Introduction to Pierre Simon Fournier,* reprint, London 1965 • **S** • SOEPNEL, INE, *Festina Lente. Aldus Manutius. Drukker / Uitgever,* Zutphen 1986 • **T** • TSCHICHOLD, JAN, *Meisterbuch der Schrift,* Ravensburg 1965 • TSCHICHOLD, JAN, *Schriften 1925 – 47,* Band I, Berlin 1991 • **V** • VERVLIET, HENDRIK D. L. / CARTER, HARRY, *Type Specimen Facsimiles,* London 1972 • VERVLIET HENDRIK D. L., *Sixteenth-Century Printing Types of the Low Countries,* London 1972 • **Z** • ZAPF, HERMANN, *ABC–XYZapf, 50 Jahre Alphabet Design; Gesammelte Beiträge über Fachliches und Persönliches für Hermann Zapf,* Offenbach 1989

3 {←} *American Copy-books* by Stanley Morison, 1951

4 {P. 127} Sign in front of the *Sir John Soanes Museum,* London

Glossary

• **TERMS** • **A** • ADVERTISING TYPEFACES: → P. 73 • **C** • CANCELLARESCA: method of cursive writing originally practiced by Vatican writing masters; later 16th-century writing masters in the promoted the style, too • CAPITALIS: (Latin for 'belonging to the head') family of ancient Roman majuscule styles, including the Capitalis Monumentalis, Capitalis Quadrata, and Capitalis Rustica → P. 17, 20, 30, 87, 106 • CAROLINGIAN MINUSCULE / CAROLINA: dominant writing style for books and charters in Western Europe from the 9th through 12th centuries → P. 17, 30, 40 • CIVILITÉ: style of printed gothic cursive type designed by ROBERT GRANJON → P. 58, 94 • CURSIVE NOMENCLATURE: italique, italic, scripts, oblique, slanted; description → P. 20 F. • **E** • ENGLISH COPPERPLATE: term for an elegant round-hand style that began to spread from England around 1750 • **F** • FRAKTUR: stringent-looking interrupted writing style that often emphasised vertical strokes → P. 18, 24, 32, 52, 64 • **G** • GREC DU ROI: Greek typeface commissioned for the King of France around 1546 → P. 56 • **H** • HALF UNCIAL: early-mediaeval book hand, which featured the first ascenders and descenders → P. 30 • HUMANISTIC SCRIPT: writing style inspired by the Carolingian Minuscule and used by the Italian Humanists → P. 32, 37 • **I** • INCUNABLE PRINTING: (from *incunabula,* Latin for 'in the cradle' or 'in infancy') first half-century or European printing with moveable type → P. 12 F. • **R** • ROMAIN DU ROI: roman and italic typefaces commissioned by the French Royal Academy of Sciences at the end of the 17th century → P. 67 • ROMAN: serif typefaces derived from ancient Roman capitals → P. 16, 18, 52, 56, 68, 74 • RONDE: French round-hand style developed around 1760 → P. 70 • ROTUNDA: round blackletter style used in Northern Italy at roughly the same time gothic architecture was en vogue → P. 24 • **S** • SLOPED ROMAN: optically slanted or otherwise cursivised version of an upright typeface → P. 23, 72, 74, 77, 79 • STYLUS: a pointed rod held in the hand and used for writing → P. 51

....

• SWASH CAPITALS: majuscule letters with in-strokes, out-strokes and tails → P. 42, 49
• **T** • TIRONIAN NOTES: method of shorthand notation from ancient Rome, attributed to Marcus
Tullius Tiro → P. 20   • **V** • VENETIAN ITALIC: the italic printing typeface produced and used by
the printer Aldus Manutius → P. 38, 46   • VERNACULAR HANDWRITING: various styles of popular
handwriting used for both informal and official purposes → P. 21

• **PEOPLE**   • **A** • ALCUIN OF YORK: (*735 York; †804 Tours) Carolingian-era educational reformer
→ P. 30   • ARRIGHI, LUDOVICO DEGLI: (*1475 Vincenza; †1527) Vatican court scribe, writing master
→ P. 12, 20, 24, 38, 40, 46, 56, 62   • **B** • BODONI, GIAMBATTISTA: (*1740 Saluzzo; †1813 Parma)
Italian punchcutter, printer → P. 70   • BRACCOLINI, POGGIO: (*1380 Terranuova; †1459 Florence)
secretary to Pope Boniface IX → P. 32   • BROOKS, GABRIEL: (*n. n. ; †n. n.) 18th-century British
engraver → P. 70   • **C** • CHARLEMAGNE: (*748; †814 Aachen) reigned as King of the Franks from
768 A.D., crowned Roman Emperor in 800 → P. 30   • COCKER, EDWARD: (*1631; †1676) 17th-century
English engraver → P. 71   • DE COLINES, SIMON: (*Gentilly; †c. 1546) French punchcutter, printer
→ P. 53   • CRESCI, GIOVANNI FRANCESCO: (*n. n. Milan; †1614) Italian writing master → P. 63
• **D** • DWIGGINS, WILLIAM ADDISON: (*1880 Martinsville; †1956 Hingham) American book designer,
graphic designer, illustrator, type designer and typographer   • **E** • ERMELER, GUSTAV FRIEDRICH:
(*n. n. ; †n. n.) German engraver active around 1820 → P. 73   • **F** • FOURNIER, PIERRE SIMON:
(*1712 Paris; †1768) French punchcutter → P. 70   • FROBEN, JOHANN: (*1460 Hammelburg; †1527
Basel) printer and punchcutter → P. 42   • FRUTIGER, ADRIAN: (*1928 Unterseen; †2015 Bremgarten
bei Bern) Swiss type designer → P. 79, 106   • **G** • GARAMOND, CLAUDE: (*1499 Paris; †1561 Paris)
French punchcutter and printer → P. 56, 112   • GILL, ERIC: (*1882 Brighton; †1940 Uxbridge) British
sculptor, stone carver, type designer and typographer → P. 77–79   • GRANJEAN DE FOUCHY,
PHILIPPE: (*1666 Mâcon; †1676) French punchcutter → S. 67   • GRANJON, ROBERT: (*1513; †1589
Rome) French punchcutter, printer → P. 56–61, 68, 101   • GRIFFO, FRANCESCO: (*1450 Bologna; †1518
Bologna) printer, punchcutter → P. 36, 38, 56   • GRYPHIUS, SEBASTIAN: (*1492 Reutlingen; †1556
Lyon) printer and bookseller → P. 42   • **H** • HAULTIN, PIERRE: (*c. 1510; †1587) French punchcutter
→ P. 60   • HOCHULI, JOST: (*1933 St. Gallen) Swiss typographer and book designer → P. 73
• **J** • JANNON, JEAN: (*1580 Switzerland; †1658) punchcutter, printer, active in Sedan and Paris
→ P. 56   • **M** • MANUTIUS, ALDUS: (*1450 Sermoneta; †1515 Venice) Venetian scholar and printer,
important representative of Italian Humanism → P. 16, 34, 56   • MEIER, HANS EDUARD: (*1922
Horgen; †2014 Obstalden) Swiss typographer and type designer → P. 79   • MOREAU, PIERRE: (*1697
Paris; †1759) French punchcutter → P. 65   • MORISON, STANLEY: (*1889 Wanstead; †1967 London)
British typographer and typographic historian → P. 35, 48, 57, 70, 74, 78   • **N** • NICCOLI, NICCOLÒ:
merchant, scholar, calligrapher (*1363; †1437 Florence) → P. 32   • **P** • PALATINO, GIAMBATTISTA:
(*1515 Rome; †1575 Naples) prominent Italian writinng master → P. 51   • PETRARCA, FRANCESCO:
(*1304 Arezzo; †1374 Arquà Petrarca) poet, important representative of Italian Humanism → P. 32, 38
• PLANTIN, CHRISTOPH: (*1520 Saint-Avertin; †1589 Antwerp) influential 16th-century printer
and publisher → P. 56, 58, 60, 64   • **S** • SALUTATI, COLUCCIO: (*1331 Stignano; †1406 Florence)
Humanist and Florentine chancellor → P. 32   • SMEIJERS, FRED: (*1961 Eindhoven) Dutch type
designer and typographer   • **T** • TAGLIENTE, GIOVANNANTONIO: (*n. n.; †1528) influential Italian
writing master → P. 22F., 46, 48   • TSCHICHOLD, JAN: (*1902 Leipzig; †1974 Locarno) German
typographer and book designer → P. 60, 82   • **U** • UNGER, GERARD: (*1942 Arnhem; †2019 Bussum)
Dutch typographer and type designer → P. 82, 100   • **V** • VAN KRIMPEN, JAN: (*1892 Haarlem; †1958)
Dutch typographer and type designer → P. 79, 82   • VESPASIANO, FRANCISCAN: (*1582; †1622 Italy)
Italian writing master → P. 62

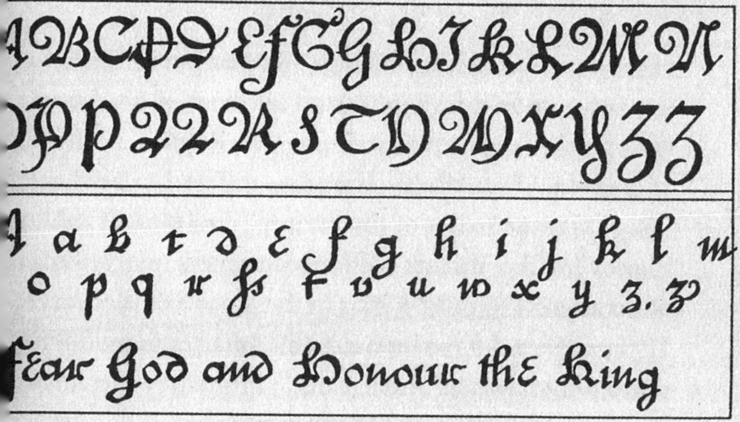

FIG. 6. *Franklin's Gothic Secretary.*

Young Man's Best Companion, containing Instructions for Reading, Writing and Arithmetic and Many other things besides the Art of making several sorts of Wines. Benjamin Franklin committed this frank piece of piracy under the imprint of Franklin & Hall in 1748. It was a well-known English manual, and the word "American" had no part in the original title. The first London edition, which I have not been able to see, was published in 1725. The many American editions of *The Instructor* that followed upon Franklin & Hall's carefully retained the several specimens of handwriting that had originally been offered to the youth of England, and in the editions of Isaiah Thomas and others the plates were closely similar to those in the English editions. Benjamin Franklin's edition was an

[17]

SIR JOHN SOANES
MUSEUM
Open Tuesday-Saturday
10 AM ~ 5 PM
ADMISSION FREE
6-9 pm on the first Tuesday
of the month
Groups must book in advance
TEL: 020-7405-2107

Lecture tour on Saturday 11·00
Tickets £5. limited to 22
available from 10·30

Special thanks

I would like to express my heartfelt thanks to all those who supported me with advice and deeds while I undertook to put this book together, as well as those who lent me their knowledge, their time or even their hearts. In many ways, each gave me certainty, strength and motivation. I would also like to thank everyone whose interesting conversations enriched my research and encouraged me to pursue interdisciplinary directions.

My particular thanks goes out to:
Sandra Ellegiers, Dan Reynolds, Fred Smeijers, Paulina Pysz, Alexander Roth, André Grau for the content and artistic support. Thanks as well my familiy, my parents Monika and Wolfgang Weber, as well as to Sophia, Leonie and Anouk.